FOOLIES A

How to change the world with a foolish dream and zero in your pocket

By Alex "Nemo" Hanse

TABLE OF CONTENTS

SPECIAL DEDICATIONS

To my beautiful mommy.

I love you so much.

You have been gone for quite some time, but your lessons are still with me.

I thank God for you.

I thank God for your joy.

I thank God for just your very existence.

I will be the Husband and the Man of God that you trained me up to be.

To the Freshman Crew, Apoc, friends, homies/homegirls, Bruhs,

Phirst Pham, Preview Staffers,

PAACT PPV's,

and all the different people I met during my UF days

I can't thank you enough for all of your support.

You are literally the reason for this company growing to where

It has grown to today.

I could be and should be giving shout outs to sooooo many people.

But, that would be tough. This list would be the entire book if I ever did a complete shout out.

So just know, I care about any and everyone who is reading this at the moment.

To Kim and Chazney.

You both are Godsends.

Thank you for being integral parts of this movement.

These two dope women give this company life.

Thank you, God, for putting all these "crazy" ideas on my heart.

Thank you for giving me a heart and spirit like my mom.

To just want to make the people around me smile and forget about

The troubles that tomorrow brings.

I hope to never lose that spirit to encourage others.

Thank You.

Let this book be used to honor you and not to gloat or highlight me.

Use my story as a light that will shine for others.

Peace

NOT YOUR AVERAGE PRELUDE

How did I write this book with a Full-Time job, running a business, and working for clients all at the same time? Clients? Yes, I started doing photography and videography for people after I finished graphic design school. (I started helping brands where Black Women were the CEO's and said how can I help them win...But that is another story for another time).

Oh yeah, I was writing this book I was also in school Full-Time as well.

So, if you don't read anything else take everything I am about to share with you to heart. I don't think you will often see this being shared, but I mean, why the heck not?

Here is the hack:

First, I wrote the table of Contents. Which you will see below.

Then, I wrote out what each chapter would be about based on the titles I came up with. Then, I used any available time I had to write using Google documents. I used my lunch breaks. I used my bathroom breaks (I know, that doesn't sound cool...). Anytime I walked to a new location or anywhere instead of texting I would add one or two more lines to my book before texting or watching. I would even just set out dedicated writing time. 20-30 minutes. I didn't want to overwhelm myself. Plus, I get hella anxiety. So, I couldn't do it to myself. And I did this for a few months straight. I was able to finish this book before a year and change.Sorry I can't give you an exact time length.

But the Table of Contents is the hack. Now, someone else may say but Nemo I am not a good writer.

That's cool...Neither am I! So, I apologize if you find any typos in here. Even my homies who helped me edit may have just gotten tired of editing because of finding so many. I had Grammarly on and Google docs has corrections too. But, you can also dictate your book. Use otter.ai. It's a website. When you talk it transcribes it, Boom! We all have writers block. But talking block is a rarity. I remember hearing that from Seth Godin in an interview. Took that advice to heart. Even though surprisingly, I didn't do that for this book. This book was burning a hole in my heart though. So once I decided to do it. I got laser focused. That's it.

Here is The Real: I've known for years that I've been too silent. I've studied this business stuff inside and out forward and backwards. But, I didn't feel like I deserved to say anything. I didn't feel like I put in enough chips to cash out just yet. This also isn't my first book. First book to be printed. But, not the first. Some people heard about it and others didn't. You would think I would promote it a few more times over...NOPE! Didn't feel like I deserved to waste your time. Crippling ain't it? I've been on panels, spoken at conferences, and in those moments I am hi-fived and applauded...But once again, still not feeling deserving or worthy because I don't have a million dollar business just yet or tons of followers and fame to show for it.

I would get asked over and over when will you write your book?

When will you throw your own conference? Why don't you stream more about this stuff? Why aren't you stepping out there and speaking up...You know so much...Do I? Funny, I live by a quote that goes: How are you a genius if no one ever knows?

Yeah, and even with that quote I still sit frozen. Well I can blabbity bla bla you with more of my issues but you get it. You go through the same battles each and every single day as well.

So what are you waiting on homie? You know what you need to be doing and so you should close this book and get to it. I appreciate the purchase. But you don't need anymore reminders.

For anyone else who goes further then I appreciate every line and every chapter you reach. Some moments I wrote with tears filled in my eyes and having to duck out of the office. Some moments I couldn't even finish a chapter because I was like dang, did I really say that? Did I really put myself out there like that? This Prelude is also being written after I wrote the book in its entirety. But that's all I got for you. I love you and appreciate you taking this journey with me. I wish I could give you more. And I plan to.

This book is the beginning of what I want to do for the world around me. This book is also my love letter to young black men and women all around the world as well. I love you and could do

nothing without your support that goes deeper than the sales. The calls, the encouragement, lifting me up when I felt like I couldn't do any of this. This is for the young brother who is being bullied for being a nerd. This is for the young queen who

has been told she was too dark and not beautiful. This is for the

bookworm. For the Oreo kid who listens to alternative rock/rock/etc. This is for the reader who grew up with no mother

or father figure. This is for the latchkey kid. This is for the kid in

the hood with the wicked jump shot. This is for the black girl who

can't stop gaming and cosplaying. People can break you physically, but can't shake your mental. They can take a lot from

you but can't take your knowledge away. And you will soon realize that your mind and your creativity is the most powerful

tool that you will have in your possession. Never stop dreaming. I still got bigger dreams...I still want to fund black films. I wanna make sure the messages we see on TV is a reflection of us in our purest form and not the watered down stuff. Tyler Perry kind of beat me to it...but it doesn't mean there can't be another right? I wanna help more black women and conquer the boardroom. So once again, this book is the beginning...I digress.

CHAPTER:-1

THE MAN BEHIND FOOLIES

Before the Gary Vaynerchuk feature...

Before the Essence and Own Network Feature...

Before Foolies...

Before Full Sail...

Before the rapping and trying to be the next Big Sean or the (old) Kanye

Before Alpha Phi Alpha

Before UF

Before being called Nemo and wearing the backpack...

We go all the way back to the streets of T double D. The home of the Dolphins and The Heat. Before D Wade my inspiration came from Alonzo Mourning and Tim Hardaway. I take you back to the days when I wore baggy white tees, Girbaud Jeans, and Gangster Rees (Reeboks). I had golds in my mouth before I had goals in my mouth (a variation of a line from my Frat Joe Clark). I was beating on desktops with plastic hair picks and pens and freestyling every time I got the chance. I had braids, plats in my head, and even a few Bob Marley tees. Interesting enough I've never smoke nor drank a day in my life...I'll explain why shortly...

While that side of me with the plats and braids came about later I was a little different when I was younger...

I had a crazy passion for dancing and acting as a kid. And of course, with acting and dancing comes a little bit of singing as well. I used to sing all the time in elementary school before puberty kicked in, of course. I remember performing the song THE TWIST by Chubby Checker:

"C'Mon baby

let's do the twist

C'mon baaabbbaaayyyy

let's do the twist

Take me by my little hand

And go like this"

I was moving and doing my thing and I had never felt a rush so amazing as seeing everyone cheer and celebrate. I was for sure I was going to be an actor and performer. Growing up I was in love with Gregory Hines. That brother was the smoothest. He even tapped danced. I was mesmerized. I knew that could be me. I mean, he even had hair like mines and everything. I was like wow, there is someone who is living out their dreams...I wanna do that...As I grew older those thoughts always stayed in the back of my mind.

Later on, the next inspiring thing I laid eyes on was the Hip Hop Kids. Do they still even exist? If you don't know about them it was one of those dance companies/troupes that you would put your kid in growing up and they would do performances all over the state and probably around the country. I could never afford the classes when I was a kid so I figured maybe I could just make up for those things in college or something.

But then all of those amazing fantasies came to an end one evening…

The sun was setting and I had just finished playing basketball for a few hours with my neighbors sons. He had two of them. After the game was over we got some juice from his pops

walked me to the door so that he can lock it after I left. For a second he stopped me…

Mr Neighbor: "Alex, you getting ready to go to college soon, right? What you gonna do in college?"

Me: "Well Sir, I was thinking about being a Theatre major! I've always had a love for acting and performing and I think it would be something I would be really great at." I had so much excitement in my soul and I was finally happy to share it with someone because no one had ever asked me before.

He looked at me with a plate of disgust that night. A feeling that I had never felt before.

Mr. Neighbor: "Theatre??!?! But you are really good at

basketball and you wrestle as well, right? Why would you do theatre?!?!" I believed he sighed and went inside and I walked back over to the place I lived in.

I think that night was the first time I questioned what I wanted to do and later on would end up changing my mind about that dream. I looked up to him. I didn't want to lose his respect for me.

But that's just one part of the story. To really give you an idea of ME as a person let me give you some info on my parentals.

If you haven't guessed by now, or don't know me, I was raised in the M-I-A streets. Born and raised in the county of Dade is what you would say if you ran into me or any of my homies from that time. 87 baby. And you know what they say about those 87 babies? Oh, you don't know? Well, they say they are the best to do it!! So take that!!

Son to two beautiful Jamaican parents. My pops name will be K for this story. My Moms name is Jackie. I used to get sent off to Jamaica every summer as a kid. My mom wanted me to appreciate what I had in the states and that's why she did it. Imagine this: You are ready to take a shower and your auntie points to a shed outside in the backyard? The water was ice cold and next to what they call a gully. Think like a big valley or something. That's where the grooming began.

Going to Jamaica each summer was so eye opening. My cousins would want me to bring them things like socks. And they were in love with all my old video games and toys. In my head I wondered why you would like or even want my hand me downs...but to them, it was a little bit closer to the dream. I imagined they looked at this as what living in the states and the land of the "free" really felt like.

The same thing that I thought was torturing me as a child was now humbling me. It was teaching me to value everything that you have. Why? Because you never know when it could all be gone or destroyed! The things I thought was unimportant may have extreme value to someone else with nothing. Someone always wants to switch shoes with you.

That was the beginning of Foolies. Before I even knew it. I mentioned I didn't drink or smoke didn't I? Yes, I did. My mom was a brilliant artist. She could draw like nobody's business. I remember being envious of her skills and stop drawing because she was so much better than me. My dad was an amazing chef and worked at a hotel for years. Before that he worked on cruise ships. Which probably explains the 12 brothers and sisters I have but have never met. And to be honest, I don't know what I would do if I did meet them. And at this point how would I even know if they were really telling me the truth as to who they are. Kinda sucks...but I try to suppress those feelings.

On my mom's side I had one brother and one sister. We all have different fathers. Interesting set up, but hey, it is what it is.

My mom and dad were divorced (not on paper). Was never sure as to why but later I would discover that my mom used to get beat by my pops. I remember her saying he used to be drunk while in the act. From that point I swore I would never be like him. I promised to never smoke, or drink, and God willing I am given the strength and peace to never get so upset in an altercation that I need to put my hands on my future wife.

All tough things to swallow at the time...

I thought she didn't love me or care for me. But it stung in my soul to find out that she was diagnosed with breast cancer. In the 90s there weren't really all these cures and health practices like they have now. I think she didn't want me to see her in the height of it all. Might have been tough for a mother to be weak in front of her baby boy. She was the pillar of the family. So I could imagine how much it hurt her, but it was for the best, I am sure.

All prepping me for who you see today. What steps will I be willing to take even if they hurt to take care of the ones I love? And every sacrifice won't be pretty but it has to be done.

Sidenote, before she passed she played Madonna's Ray of Light every day. So that album means a lot to me. You know what's crazy though? I wish I could have a video rolling of me typing this stuff and tearing up. I've never really shared all of this with anyone.

One more sidenote: Freeport (the area in Bahamas that I stayed in) had the prettiest and bluest oceans ever. And goombay punch is legit the best soda ever in all of life! It's a pineapple soda that is amazing. But why Bahamas? My mom was dating a usician at the time and his family stayed there. They didn't work out. But that's another story to not even get into. He was like a pops for me at the time. We don't speak much now a days.

But I was thankful he was around. He jump started my passion for music. He was in a reggae band and some nights the band would let me come to the shows and play the wood blocks or the Cabasa. Had to look it up. I just called it a shaker. But yeah. He always had different artist over the house. He even showed me the popular chords for most reggae songs: F-A-C, G-B-E....I think that's what it was at least. It was a whole new world for me but it was something I wanted to be part of for sure.

Another side note: There is no mac and cheese greater than Bahamian Mac and cheese. The end.

Fast Forwarding to 6th grade. When I lost my mom, it was the day before Mother's Day. When I say tough. I meeaaaaaannnn tooooouuggghhhh. My supposed stepmom at the time told she was gonna take care of me. Weeks later she would run off with my dad's money and end up leaving him.

Sucks right? Nope.

Wait what Nemo? No, I'm sorry man, that sucks. You can't say--WAIT...

Once again, all preparation.

Life, ain't perfect.

People will break their promises.

That is their flaw. Not yours.

Moving on...

My mom actually sewed and made clothes. She quit her career as a nurse to follow her dream as a hairstylist/cosmetologist. Yo! Quick side note, hair shows are amazing. She used to take me to them as a kid. The music. The lights. The showcase as a whole. So epic. Back to the story.

One of the dopest things I remember is seeing my mom go back to school. Got her G.E.D and made it happen. She taught me through her actions to go after your dreams no matter the cost or sacrifice. Before she died, she wanted to open up her own salon. She never got that chance to do so. She had the blueprints and everything.

Another prep to the man I am today. So one of the reasons I go so hard via social and every day life is because I don't want the people I care about to leave this planet with the dream still in their hearts. It burns me up just thinking about it...And that will be the fire behind every chapter.

Here's Your Mission: What part of your life can you start sharing today? Doesn't mean go as far as sharing some deep life story, but there are points in your life that has some lessons wrapped in there. Once or twice a week I'd encourage you to share a lesson. Aht. Aht. Don't tell me nobody cares. Someone needs the gems you have to share. Once again, one or two lessons a week. Lessons from work, parents, or even a dope lesson from a movie you've watched. Your first way to change the world and not even spend a dime. If you don't like to write you can easily jump on a video and post something you've learned in the last year. If you are not going to share it via social media at least share it with your closest friend, or partner. Something you say to them can also push them to change the world around them as well. Have you ever seen a pebble thrown across a pool or a pond? Small pebble right? Usually it makes this cool ripple effect that goes across the entire pond. You can be the ripple.

Quick Freestyle:

You can never shake or BREAK ME

I remain cooler than ACs

So INNATELY

I expect a few to HATE me

And I'm gonna do it all

Because that's what I have to do

I'm still the ONE

But you go ahead and read chapter 2

Peace.

CHAPTER:-2

SHIFTING YOUR MINDSET

I wouldn't be here today

If it wasn't for Sade (Famous singer. Look her up).

When I lost my ole girl

I could have lost my way

But I thank God for getting me through this

I woulda ended my whole life if it wasn't for music...

Music gave me swagger. Music got me through tough times. Music was my escape when life got hard to music was the go to. It brought me the confidence that no one ever taught me while growing up. Hearing Jay Z made me think I could dominate the world. Listening to Eminem taught me I could be unique and different. I used to call myself Slim Shaded which I was going to be the black version of Eminem. I used to want to rap like Jay Z. I remember when I heard he didn't write his lyrics. I made a quest to never write mines down as well. I do every now and then. Just doodle lines down. But, I do my best to be like my unofficial or virtual mentor (I have a lot of virtual mentors. People I have never met but have played a role in grooming me).

The beauty of music and especially hip-hop music is it shows you that big things are attainable. I figured if these rappers could get out of their respective hoods and change the world then why can't I?

Outside of hip hop...I fell in love with an artist named Sade...

Sades album entitled Lovers Rock also saved my life. There was a song called By Your Side that I used to sing every single night. I feel like my mom's spirit and Sades thoughts were in sync.

Sings

Oh, when you're cold

I'll be there

Hold you tight to me.

Oh, when you're low

I'll be there

By your side, baby

Every single night I would just set the song on repeat and let the flashing red light on my CD player hypnotize me. What's a CD player you ask? Well, kids back in my day lol...

This song provided the healing I needed to go on.

When you have no parents raising you past the 6th grade only a few things could happen according to society for a young black man: Death or a Dropout. I remember back in elementary school I had a teacher tell me that I wasn't gonna amount to anything. Had other teachers that said I was stupid and never going to make it in life.

Outside of music there was one teacher, Mr. Tootsie Roll (I won't

use real names of people that I did not not get permission to use). Mr Tootsie Roll (or Mr. TR for short in this scenario) told me that one day I would be the first black president. That little seed did a lot for me. I actually became student government president in elementary school maybe between 4th and 6th grade. When my mom passed I wrote an essay called "The greatest gift I ever received." I made it about my mom, but I believe the prompt was more so for inanimate objects: Toys, "blankee", etc.

I made it about my mom instead it won this award thing and it was another seed that was planted that made me think that maybe if I ever wanted to write I would have a decent shot at it.

Did I also mention I was a very bad child? Oh gosh, I was the worse. A3D A3F on my report cards. I talked too much in class. I was always being rude and slick with my teachers. I meant no harm. My teachers actually loved me a lot, but just knew something was going on and I think they put 2 and 2 together that I just needed love and guidance. My mom whenever I did something wrong in school would make me write letters to the teachers and the principal or whoever the drama involved. These things harnessed my writing skills even if I don't give it the credit that it did. I did later get put in gifted classes. That was also a wild and interesting world. But another story for another day.

But my mom always saw the good in me. I always remembered her saying, "you are going to be a great husband and such an amazing man of God." She was the quintessential bible toting Jamaican woman and so she was always encouraging me and her friends. She was always the go-to for her friends. I remember being in rooms and just watching how encouraging she was and even if I didn't realize it immediately it also helped me. This is why I encourage the homies and push them and just like my mom she would call people out on their crap and she always kept it honest.

And she was so passionate about her craft of cosmetology. She introduced me to the world of hair shows. I thought it was gonna be something girlie and lame, but it was amaaaaazziinnng. Before she passed she was working on a show. She slaved over it day and night. She wanted everything to be perfect. She used Madonna's Ray of Light single for the show. I could hear the pops and clicks or the tape deck (Plukunk) and then the rewind (Vvzzzzzz). Her head was always hurting her, and I remembered seeing her slumped over the bathroom sink and toilet bowl...she knew it was her last show. We even went back to Jamaica during that time period. NORMALLY, she just sent me alone, but this time she made it a point to be there to see family. She was setting the stage and saying her final dues clearly.

Preparation for me once again...If my mom in her last year or two was still grinding and working hard despite imminent doom then why should I be doing anything less as an adult.

(Yo, side note the mosquitos in Jamaica were as big as quarters lol. I SweatuhGawd...)

My mom always said Manners will take you through the world. That was her message. Even though I was a bad kid it was only for a short season. I wanted attention. I needed a Male figure. I almost ended up joining some mini gang for a bit. But when my mom passed I couldn't do anything but stop and think about all of her lessons. It made me get right and pick myself up from sobbing. Now I live like she was still over my shoulder.

Losing her was the worst thing on the planet earth to me. I knew from that point I could only go up and I knew at a young age that I am supposed to be a value to someone else. Didn't know when it would be but I also knew that I didn't want my mom in pain and alive just to appease me. I did not go to the hospital the night she passed. Something didn't feel right hours before. Then later that evening I found out. I later heard people were arguing over worldly possessions of hers and what to do with me. That also made me upset but once again, at least she was in peace now. My mom was selfless even up until her last breath. So I couldn't be anything else than that.

Everything happens for a reason right? There's a quote I

remember hearing that said: How could the worst moment of

your life be spun or used as the best thing that has ever happened to you? I urge you to find the blessing in the toughest of times. It will do you a world of good.

Here's Your Mission: Think about a moment in your life that was pretty bad. Were there any lessons that you could take from it? Now, I know you may not want to. But could you? If the answer is yes, then write down what that lesson is right now on a sheet of paper, or in the notes section of your phone. Screenshot it and tag @Foolies on IG. Simple way to make an impact. Shifting your mindset won't be fun. But it will shake things up for someone I promise.

CHAPTER:-3

THE POWER OF BEING NAIVE

A lot of time was a blur after my mom passed. The only real vivid years may have been bits and pieces of middle school, bits and pieces of high school, but really the heart of who I am formed when I got to college.

And college is where the movement or mission of Foolies came to life. Well, after I finished college at least. But still throughout college too…alright, you get me.

(Side note: I did create this brand when I was a kid called the J-Walkerz. I knew I wasn't a thug per se, so I figured this would be a line of t-shirts for people who want to be in that life but don't wanna be in that life at all kind of deal. It was silly. But I drew it out and everything. I would hold my hands up making a J yelling out J WALKERZ!! In hopes to sound rather intimidating. Just another prequel to the dream later).

But how could an Applied Physiology and Kinesiology grad build a clothing line? That was my major back at my first alma mater, The University of Florida. The best school in the entire wooooooorrrld!! Slightly biased but it is what it is. If you are a Seminole reading this right now I hope you stub your big toe. Yep, I live in the spirit of petty. To anyone else who doesn't know FSU is a school we have despised since the dark ages.

But once again the question remains... How could an Applied

Physiology and Kinesiology grad build a clothing line? (I'll explain this major and why I took it up and how I ended up becoming an audio engineer and graphic designer later, I promise)

Good freaking question. Hahha. I don't know how I did it. I've always simplified things in my head. Okay, well, if I want to make t-shirts I would make a design and then find someone who can print it right? Sounded simple in my head.

And to be honest me not knowing anything about how to start a business was the best mindset for Foolies. I feel like sometimes when you are too smart you psych yourself out of things.

Oh, btw, before we get too far, Foolies are people who are so driven and motivated to live out their goals and dreams that they are called "FOOLS" for trying to do so.

Back to It

The approach to this t-shirt thang (yes, thang) has been a very foolish endeavor. Why so, Sir Nemo? Well, I knew nothing about fashion. I knew nothing about T-shirts. I knew nothing about having an online website. I knew absolutely nothing about anything. It was me and my brother from another mother and skin color Billy Kennedy. I was the rapper and he was the engineer. I imagined that every rapper had a clothing line (especially in the 2000s) so why not? It gives the fans something to purchase after you rock out at a show. Now, before this I remember doing a google search: HOW DO RAPPERS BUILD A BRAND? I don't remember the name of the website that I found, but here is the ONE gem it gave me:

Create an identity for your fan base. If they know who they are, they know what to latch on to. Lady Gaga has her little monsters or something like that. Wiz Khalifa had the Taylor Gang or Die movement growing. Even though it wasn't a "group" or identity per se, Big Sean would say "WHOA DERE." When Lil Wayne came on a track during that time you would hear a lighter flicker. This was all part of the brand association to give the audience something to look forward to.

I played around with a few words and concepts. Then I think I said something like "This is foolish of us man." That "foolish" quote evolved to "Foolies" and here we are. But why did we think about the word "FOOLISH.." The context for that was I was a college grad from the University of Florida (GO GATORS!!) and Billy was graduating in a few years. We weren't in any majors that necessarily screamed "creative" per se. He was Journalism (If my memory serves me correctly) and I was Applied Physiology and Kinesiology with a specialization in Fitness and Wellness. Bum Bum Bum!! Or Dun Dun Dun!!! Whatever that sound is when the plot thickens *rubs hands like birdman.* As I said, I KNEW NOTHING ABOUT THIS BUSINESS BEFORE I STARTED.

But that is why it has grown to be so successful (at least in my opinion :-)). Now, over the years through CreativeLive (Josh Kaufman Personal MBA was a game changer course) courses and thousands of hours of Youtube, Seth Godin Books, studying celebrities and their moves they have made and ALSO grabbing their books, Gary Vee Content, being a volunteer for an amazing organization called 1 Million Cups and just my own personal highs and lows has taught me so much about business. You would think I had like 3 MBA's from Wharton or something with all the knowledge I have gained over the years.

I didn't pay attention to all the stupid stats like most businesses fail in the first five years. Or that small businesses don't last and the other narratives out there. Therefore, when we fell into seasons where we were "failing" we just pivoted and made a change to the company. Foolies doesn't have rules like the big players in the game have. So we can pivot and shift as much as possible. It was funny moments where there were no sales coming in or any real traction for Foolies I said stuff like, "let's give the people more!!" What the heck kind of concept is that? The investors I am sure would have laughed at me heavily had they heard that. Yep, that was what started the letters, the paint cans, and me making videos for my customers and songs via SoundCloud. I was calling customers personally and thanking them. Throwing in extra T-shirts, wristbands, and anything I could do to make it all happen. I remember presenting this concept at an event and they told me, "How does that scale?" A lot of fake shark tank people out there thinking they know everything. "What happens when you get too many orders." My response: "Then I will adjust. And that is a great problem to have, so a way will be made." To be honest, I was peacocking lol! Had no clue as to what I was going to do, but I knew one thing: I will NOT lose. Too much on the plate. Too much at steak (get it?). I'm a wrapper/rapper, so you have to expect each word I give will be a gift! (Did you get that one? Hahha! I can do this all day).

So here is what I did for a few years with foolies.

This is me tapping into my inner Disney vibes...

Check it...

yells Alright kids gather around

As I tell the tale of Foolies

This story may be simple

But quite enchanting

and even moving

Every customer would get a t-shirt inside of mini paint can. A handwritten letter would be inside too. Then I included wrist bands and other swag if I could with the orders. Back then that was expensive, but it was worth it. Customers would post pics of their letters more than their t-shirts. They would text me or email me or even call me back (most of my first customers and still are my friends) in tears. Not knowing that what I wrote aligned to where they were in life at the moment. I was being more than a t-shirt company, and I didn't even know it. Most times while writing I'd be in tears myself. Just because some of the letters felt like they were dedications to myself. If you order today things are not the same. Everything goes through Teespring (I'll explain this process a little more later) being that I started gaining way more customers than I could handle. Plus, I also work full time, so I had to find an easier way to make it all work. I was doing a lot of the packaging and shipping for a few years and that was rough. I wore down my car. I was so freaking hungry because I wasn't really making much. I was picking up dead-end jobs and writing on Fiverr to make ends meet. I was still doing my freelance thing on the audio side of my second degree I obtained from Full Sail so that was a saving grace. I also did a short season as a tutor for a middle school and worked at the Boys and Girls club as well. Anything to help fund the dream.

Another sidenote:

You know what is funny? The brand once sold "stay natural" shirts back before the movement really grew. I got virtually stoned. What about the straight hair folk? Folks with perms? Etc. Mind you this was before the push for natural really was making a way into our everyday lives. What does this mean?

Pro tip: TRUST YOUR GUT. They may not understand what you are doing now, but you know what it will be later.

Now, I think the naive thing I did at the beginning of Foolies was assuming that the brand was for "EVERYONE!" Whenever anyone asked me about who my target market was (because I didn't know what that meant at the time) I would say foolish things like "Dancers, singers, Teachers, black, blue, purple, and anyone with a dream in their heart."

Silly me! Hey everyone, your brand isn't for everyone. If Coca Cola wants to target 19-year-old white men starting college in a school that is along the SEC theme of things (UF, UGA, TENNESSEE ETC) then they will pour all of their efforts into targeting that group. Doesn't mean Coca-Cola doesn't want other people latching on to their product, but they know who they are after and they are sticking to it. It is okay to have an idea of who your brand is for. If other people buy in the process, that means what you are doing is WORKING! Brand Spillage is what I will dub the term as. It is basically the essence of HIP HOP music today. Started by people of color and now it is loved and accepted by the world. I also had to understand that my brand is whatever people say it is. It has nothing to do with what I am jotting down or what my mission statement is on my website. If people say my brand is for old people, or for young millennials, or dope African American woman I can either tailor to that or start creating a better messaging around my brand, so people don't get confused. I had to find myself. I thought I should sell to everyone. I had this narrative programmed in my head that "Black people don't support their own." And would be littered by concepts like "Black people don't support their homeboy/homegirl but they support Beyonce." False narratives like that messed me up in the early stages. From the beginning of the brand until now Black Women have been the driving force behind what I do. So why stray away from who is pushing me and helping me succeed? I wanted to do focus heavily on black women from the beginning, but I didn't trust my gut even though all the signs were there that a movement was growing, and they would need that support.

Don't let anyone make you feel bad about who you want to focus on in regards to your company. If others get upset, then oh freaking well. KNOW YOUR MARKET. UNDERSTAND WHERE HOME IS. Focus their first and then evolve the brand as you go forward. You all do know the ads in Italy for Nike and America will be different right? They will put Messi on a graphic in Brazil to promote a shoe and Lebron on another here in the states, you do know this right? Now, this doesn't mean be shady and market yourself differently where other eyes can't see. It just means don't go selling your vegan pops at the Carnivore Conference for Steak Eating Burger Operators and be mad that you are not making a single sale.

And to be even clearer: A breakdown of who Foolies thinks about when creating content, apparel etc.

Foolies Customer Psychographics

My customer is between 24 & 31.

African American Woman

She is a graduate from a Journalism School.

Loves art. Loves traveling. Loves family and her alma mata.

She's a grad from an HBCU (Historically Black College or University) or was heavily involved in the black community at her PWI (Predominantly White Institution).

She grew up in Atlanta.

Went to Howard.

Now lives in New York and secured a job as multimedia journalist for a growing brand agency.

Her problem at the moment: She isn't seeing her purpose and is being tugged towards running her own company, or just needs a company that supports her and cares for her more. Her income annually is 30K and she hopes to change that with some entrepreneurial endeavors that she will be digging into.

I have created an entire life for the market I want to focus on. You should as well. How can my brand push and motivate someone if I don't even know who I am doing this for?

Give your audience a name.

An Idea.

A concept worth believing in.

Then whatever that is make sure it is in the messaging over and over and over again. For you it will get tiring and boring. But someone hasn't seen you yet. Before the sales come in people have to know what they are getting into. What are they connecting to? Who are they supporting? We don't just buy blindly anymore. That is why you see more of ME in the brand than ever. 7 years back I would just post pictures of shirts or girls in shirts. Not me.

All in all, this came with time, my friends. But if it wasn't for my naivety I wouldn't even have been able to write this very book I am writing for you. I have written a book in the past and when I was writing it someone said, "Alex, you will never be able to get it published...I know the industry--" Those are the words of someone who doesn't know me. Plus, real friends don't call me Alex anyways YA BASTARD hahah! I kid. I kid. But, I figured out online publishing methods. Created a kindle publishing account and BOOM! I made it a free E-Book. Shots of Espresso: Motivational Thoughts to Pick You Up. I took blog content and FB posts and made it into a book. That simple? Why was it that simple? Cause I was naive while doing it all. I was determined to make it happen one way or another and I did. And when I have doubts the two G's always gets me through. God & Google! Let the church say, AMEN! I do mean it! Go find my book post on my @Foolies page and say AMEN in the comments section. Tell me you just finished the 3rd chapter and I am doing as instructed hahah!

Here's Your Mission: Go to a local Starbucks. Take a pen and pad with you. You have a few things you can do here. You can pen a letter about the power or living out your dreams. Then, find an unsuspecting soul and pass them the letter and leave. That's it. Free 99. I've done this on many occasions. Your letter may be different. But, you get the point. It could be words of encouragement or an even simpler message like: Be Kind To Yourself.

Another thing you can do that is pretty easy. Go to Teespring.com. Put a quote that inspires you on a T-shirt. Order

the shirt for yourself. Then wear the shirt when you go places. Trust me, someone is going to be impacted. It's also a great conversation starter as well. Now that might cost you like $20 bucks. But it could go a very long way.

CHAPTER:-4

CHAMPAGNE DREAMS, KOOL-AID MONEY

If you are like me you have Champagne Dreams and Kool-Aid Money. This means you have humongous ideas and very little capital to do so. Well, how did Foolies start without any capital? Well, I will tell you.

It was time!

We (me and my co-founder) didn't know how it was going to be done, but we figured how do we get the idea for the shirt off the ground? Well, let's get T-shirts printed and get them to all of our friends? But one small problem. Printing T-Shirts cost. And me and Billy both were broke as a joke. There was one album we put out together called, "Turn off the Radio." And on the song entitled Turn Off The Radio on that album, I talk about what I was trying to do to get into the rap game. Emailing blogs constantly. Sending them our singles via mp3 or Youtube or whatever means we had. And we didn't know any other way to get on other than sending our music to blogs and anyone who had a buzz. And we got a couple features. Some big, some small. So I figured all I have to do for this brand is make the product and then start getting it on the backs of people in the same way we did the music. See, the music game was inspiring the T-shirt hustle all along.

Also, going back to my hay days of selling chips and juice in high school. I would go to a corner store or Arab store as we called back in the hood. Apologies about the name that is just what we called it. I really want to be authentic as I share this stuff so it may not all be politically correct.

Back to it...hen I went to these corner stores I would buy chips for a quarter apiece. I could then sell those same chips for 50 cents. I would double my profit as long as I wasn't getting high on my own supply kind of deal. But, it is was different. I was hungry. I ate my profits often. Especially, Hot Cheetos and honey barbeque chips. Wooooooooooo-Weeeeeeee! Anywho, I would take 5 dollars and make ten. Spend another five dollars make another ten more. Then I would say cool, let me spend this 15 dollars I have and buy that much worth of chips to make 30. Go back to spending 5. Then repeat this process. Not quite sure what I was doing, but it was semi-working. Then any money I got from friends of the family, under the couch, or doing whatever would make a kid a few bucks I would take and go buy more stuff. I would buy a pack of airheads that came with 72 in the pack. Back in the day, they were like 7 bucks. I would sell each for a quarter apiece and make back 18. Look yall, I had no clue what I was doing, but it was working! Then, me and a few homeboys who were all selling chips and juice decided to go all in together at some point. We had 4 huge duffle bags on the court where everyone would play basketball in the morning time. We were literally like a storefront. I sold sporting cards, I sold literal mixtapes, and so much other random crap. I just know I couldn't sell drugs. I'm sure I could have. But, I was too scared to get into selling weed or doing anything like that. If I got with a couple hundred airheads on me I figured I could negotiate my way out of that a little easier (laughs to self). Plus, I didn't want to let my mom down. Also, I was staying with a good friend of the family at the time and she had about 10 plus kids in the house including me and for a short period of time my pops as well. I wanted to take the burden off of her. So I was trying to make ends meet however I could.

Eventually, I would get a job at the car wash! Rest in peace to the owner. He passed away. While I didn't like the guy sometimes I knew he wasn't bad at heart. Jamaican dude. He lost his life trying to stop a lady from being robbed from what I heard. So rest in peace my dude and thanks for giving me my first semi-real job. I would make $3 per car $5 per truck. Bruh, I would come up on a good $200+ on a Saturday. That is me adding in tips as well. The goal was to provide as much value as I could for each driver in hopes to get a fat tip. Sometimes it sucked when it was only like $1 or when people didn't have anything to give. I had to realize that in life sometimes you will go above and beyond and you have to truly control your intentions behind what you do else you will be butt booty hurt all the time.

Then I grew up some more when I got my first job at Wendy's. I remember walking in every day and asking the simple question: "Can I speak to your manager?" That was the indication that I wanted to ask the boss about a job. That was also in the era of filling out paper applications as well! Pretty crazy to think about how I never filled out an application again. But outside of the "back in my day" talk it really humbled me and it forced me to figure out the words to say when I didn't always know what to say. It helped me build up confidence and overcome my fears of asking the tough questions.

So wait, Nemo? What does all of this have to do with Foolies?

Can't you see it by now? I had to get scrappy to survive. Why would I do anything less for this business? So, how did we finally get a shirt off the ground? Well, me and billy said let's take an old dirty white shirt we already had and go to Walmart. We would procure this kind of printing paper that you could then iron on a shirt. Billy had an inkjet printer--Excuse me, A LASER INKJET PRINTER! We ironed the word on a shirt and then I

would wear it to my performances whenever I got them. Oh, ya

boy opened up for Big Krit and Curren$y back in the day. Also, God rest his soul, but I was a host for a Mac Miller concert as well back in my UF days. And in those moments, of course, guess what shirt I was wearing? My Foolies shirt of course. What is crazy is that I see people with T-shirt brands and they don't even wear their own apparel. If you are not rocking your own brand why would anyone else?

When we only had one shirt we would also make our other friends put it on and wear it. Take a picture. Take it back. Look yo, we had to make it work. I couldn't be printing shirts and getting them to the masses. Didn't even know at the time where the heck you find a T-Shirt printer so once again, we had to make it work. We found this T-Shirt site called Reverbnation or at least Billy found it. It was for artists back in the day to get their name out. It was a music website. But they had a portion where the artist could sell merch. Those were fun times but the product was mad janky and printed on these weak behind Hanes tees. Hanes and Gildan might be the worst. But, they are the most affordable. So go for what you know!

Before long I would have my friends saying, "I WANT ONE!" And in my head, I'm like, "YOU DO?!" Sure! But, I had to also be a big advocate for my brand. I would yell FOOOOLIIIEESSS all throughout my music and make sure I was inconvenient places with my product on. The beauty is you guys don't even have to do all this mess I had to do to get on. You can literally make a free account to print shirts via Teespring and start your T-Shirt business tonight! They will ship it and cut you a profit. You probably can't find time to talk to a t-shirt printing store to print shirts like I did back in 2011 and you probably can't afford to be quitting your job like I did around 2012 and be shipping people shirts in fancy cans and writing letters. Once again, what the heck did I know about business? I was wasting tons of money just to make people happy.

I quickly interrupt your reading to give a shout out to all the people who allowed me to crash on their couches when I was in the struggle: Swain & Wali, T (a.k.a froggy) and Glass Menagerie

(You know who you are and Kenny too. I still have you in my phone as my roommate, and all the people who randomly called me and took me out to lunch, who sent me a Publix gift card in the struggle, and the list of shout outs go on and on...Shouts out to my frat AK who got me my first few hundred bucks to go buy a bulk order of shirts from a local printer in town. Shouts out to another frat Ken who said "you know what, I see what you are doing here are a few more hundred bucks to buy another bulk order of tees." Some investments I had to pay back when I got the money. Others were gifted to me. Appreciate you Alton for helping me and making a quick investment in me as well and the brand. Ken, you too man. You saw things in the brand that was worth something. Thank you as well for the help many years ago.

Now back to your reading

But Imagine if I would have quit? People saw me breaking my back and putting it all on the line and finally, someone saw it was worthy to just pass me a couple hundreds (and when I say a couple, I mean a couple lol) to make it to the next destination. It wasn't some million-dollar investment, but it inspired me that If I could keep going more successful things would come out of it all.

How I started all of this was pure finesse. A lot of luck. A lot of prayers. And a lot of networking. A whole heap of it. A decade-plus of meeting and connecting with people was now paying off. You never know who is watching you in life so be careful my friends. Don't ever get too high and mighty and start burning bridges or thinking you are better than the next man. You never know how those same people you may have helped or who just saw you being a good person could turn around and lead to the greatest blessing you ever received. Thank you to my fave, Tiffuhknee (not how it's really spelled but you get it) who would help me out on so many occasions with the brand. But many more shoutouts will come later throughout the book as well. My rounds of applause aren't done just yet. I won't be able to shout them all out, but I will do my best.

And for you, the person reading: Young King, Queen, Melanated, or No Melanin in sight at all, whatsoever (chuckles) you have to use what you already have around you. You have to get creative. And use the stories of others to help you in your journey. The only reason I thought about putting people in shirts and taking it off after the photo op was because I remember reading that Daymond John did the very same thing back in the 90s with FUBU. Look Y'all, success leaves clues. And if you think you are going to come up with some genius concept on your own then you are pretty delusional. I've also supported people and looked out for them and prayed with them or for them, and just did my best for the people I love and care about and when they see your heart they will wish the same things for you. They will push and hope that you succeed. How I got Foolies off the ground isn't some rocket science. It's heart science. It's ambitious adrenaline. It's keeping that little voice in my head tuned to the right frequency. And when it goes off the pitch or off the mark I allow it to do so and then I reel it back in before it gets too far off the track.

Once again, you have more tools now to do the thing you love than I ever did back in the early 2000s. You got that incredible thing called the cell phone that you pay almost a month's rent for that you could be using. Want to start your bakery? Cool! Make cakes at the crib and make your friends come over to try them out. After they try them out film them giving a testimony of how great your cakes are. Want to make it in the makeup industry? Every single day you need to start posting pictures on

Instagram of you showing off how you did your eye shadow, or your mascara or those wing-tipped looking things at the corner of your eyes. Want to be a connector and make a business out of that? Start hosting dinner parties. Find a dope chef. Find a dope location: Mansion, Air BNB, HomeAway (another website that lets you rent out people's homes), a local high school gym and bring people in the room together for like 5 to 10 bucks (in the early stage) and cause dope and valuable connections to happen between the individuals who attend. Want to start that video series with all those creative ideas you have? Great! Use your cell phone and film your videos in your room. Edit on iMovie for now until you get your money up to maybe buy Adobe Premiere or Final Cut. I am an Adobe Premiere fan and would HIGHLY recommend you getting the ADOBE Suite if you can. Look, if you have to pay your buddy to come over their crib and use their MacBook pro to edit your videos then do that. Also, libraries are a HUGE untapped resource. I would start calling up your local libraries and see what kind of software and gear they have inside. In Orlando, there is a place called the Melrose Center. This freaking place has a full-on studio, photography room, 3D printing lab, and so many other things. It is free if you are a resident of Orlando. If not, I think it is like a yearly fee that isn't that much. You might have something like this as well. But no worries, I will talk about this again later in the resources section.

START GETTING SCRAPPY AND SAVVY. I've sent hundreds of emails. Dozens of DM's. Made calls. Been to dozens of networking events. I have volunteered at conferences that I couldn't afford. Look, I have to make things happen. And THE LACK OF MONEY WILL NOT STOP ME FROM GETTING TO MY GOALS AND DREAMS. I REPEAT, THE. LACK. OF. MONEY. WILL. NOT. ME. FROM. GETTING. TO. MY. DREAMS. AND. GOALS. Remember why I am here right now? It is to show you the way out. The way to your freedom. This is a modern-day underground railroad to your best life. And a lot more people would be free if they didn't realize they have set their own traps of doubt, fear, anxiety, and so much more. A lot more people would be walking in purpose if they weren't still lingering and holding on to the pain and the heartache and the partner that stole all of your money...I GET IT!! But when will you wipe the freaking tears and get back to work already? We know you are good at crying! We know you are great at sobbing. Now, as I write my story...I am blessed to be part of YOUR NEW STORY that is being formed. You have to get out of this mental funk and pass failures and LEVEL UP homies (someone pass this book on to Ciara for ya boy and told her I shouted her out by accident ;-)). Me being broke and picked on back in the day woke me up to more. I couldn't cry and complain that mommy wasn't there and that my daddy bailed on me. I had to figure it out because it was a life or death situation. This meant that if I don't live out the purpose in my LIFE I can cause the DEATH of someone who needed to meet me, or read my book, or run into one of my Foolies Fridays, or T-Shirts. The mission is locked in. That is why I can continue building this business with just me and my small team (Shouts out to Kim and Chazney. Love yall to death). You probably have a far better way to get to the top. And you probably have more that you are fighting for. And I am not telling you anything new...But sometimes we have to be reminded or activated. I watch a lot of spy shows and movies. These agents, they call them sleepers. They are normal but deep down there is something inside of them. Once the code word gets sent out they waken back up and complete their task and NOTHING will stop them. Now, SLEEPERS are not usually good guys. But in this case, it will be used. The codeword is FOOLIES APPROVED. Or, just FOOLIES. And when you see or hear those words just remember to wake up that person inside of you and tell them that the mission is on. And nothing will stop you. No matter what.

Here's Your Mission: Send an email to a friend, Co worker or management today. What kind of email you ask? Great question. Send an encouraging one. Send one that tells the person how you feel about them and all the reasons why they are so dope/cool/amazing etc. If you want to step it up then even go over to their office. Make a phone call. Yes, right now. Stop what you are doing and call someone and tell them you appreciate them. But Nemo, that can't change the world? Really? I've called people who just happened to be balling their eyes out and who knows what I did to save their lives. You can be a lifesaver as well. Don't overthink making an impact. That's the biggest mistake most make.

P.S. Wanna talk ideas? DM me on Instagram @Foolies. If there is a will there's a way. And even if your idea is a horrible one maybe there's a gem deep within the idea that can still be made into something valuable. It happens all the time. A company idea fails and then ONE part of the company remains and becomes the million-dollar idea. If I don't respond quickly then follow up. I do get more DM's than the average. So I won't deliberately ignore you unless the way you have reached out is completely rude or disrespectful. I am not a celeb or someone important, but respect is important to me. I have had people reach out in some of the weirdest of ways and in quite the rude manner as if I was SUPPOSED to message them back or just in a nasty or negative way. But, if you are reading this I imagine you are friends and family. But the disclaimer had to be set.

CHAPTER:-5

TRUE POWER = CONSISTENCY

Quick Freestyle:

How could I ever stop

This ain't about me

The only muscle I got

Is CON-SIS-TEN-CY

So every day that I do this

You should know why

Here's a few more gems

Imma give you in chapter five

Today, I am sharing with you the things I have done. I am no expert. But, I will give you a fast pass if you just want the gems and you want to be out. After you read these small steps you can choose to skip to the next chapter if you so choose. If you want context then continue reading:

Build your email list. Build your email list. Build your email list.

Learn to Copywrite.

Learn how to sell

Then learn all you can about how to become a Purple Cow. Go look it up.

Once again, this is my unique perspective and you can totally ignore anything that you don't feel is valuable to you. So here is me elaborating on my steps above.

First things first, I should have created an email list. The social media platforms won't be around forever. And sometimes, people don't care to necessarily go to your site all the time. But, one thing we all still receive on a consistent basis is emails.

So here is what I do. For the last few years I have sent daily emails to encourage my homies to live out their dreams, purpose, and/or calling and every Friday I give them a list of tools and resources and things they can use for their own business. That is the only day of the week (unless I am releasing a new shirt) where I will ask for support for my brand and for people to buy apparel.

Now in these emails, I shared my mistakes (now I share my successes). I share life lessons. I share things I don't normally post to the (insta)gram. It is a lot more intimate and I am a lot more open with that content. It is a muscle that I have built after I heard my virtual mentor explain why he writes every day.

Sidenote: Virtual Mentors are people who I have never met, but I study them and use them as a resource. If I feel like I need a quick pick me up I will watch their content, read their blogs, and books. Simple as that. I may never meet these people, but that doesn't mean I can't learn from them.

Seth Godin (one of those virtual mentors) said in an interview that the best advice he can give is to write every single day. He does it and so I do it. Building a brand and having a banging social media presence is dope. But, I should have directed my energy to creating an email list. I use Mailchimp. Feel free to use whatever you find is fitting for you. I think I would have made more money if I had focused my energy here. I have seen tens of thousands of dollars through Foolies. But, all of it would go right back into the brand. So I don't profit from any of this (just yet) and my team that helps me faithfully I can't thank them enough. But, these are the sacrifices that are needed to be made in order to be great. I work Full Time to stay afloat and then the business when I get off from work. My motto: Before Work, After Work, and on the Weekends. I feel like someone said that to me and then I added the On The Weekends part. But, who knows. I've made it one of my many life mottos.

Before starting to build your business try doing this activity first. Think about the brand, the business, the nonprofit that you are hoping to start. For instance, let's say you want to build a makeup line. You need to be asking your friends what kind of makeup do they use? Who are they watching to get makeup tips and advice? Where do they shop for makeup? What do they wish they could learn about doing their own makeup? Don't just say on your Facebook page, "Hey, should I start a makeup vlog?" While that question makes sense the most you are going to get out of people is a YES.

Get even more detailed..Ask them what makeup vloggers do they love the most? What is their favorite thing about makeup vlogs or the vlogger they mentioned? What do you wish makeup vloggers would stop doing? The list of questions could go on and on. But, I think you understand. Ask them have they ever been to a makeup party before? And not necessarily the Mary Kay stuff. Just a bunch of homies kicking it and getting their faces "beat?" Is that what they say? Am I hip now?!?!? ***Does Milly Rock on every block.*** And you can do this same thing for sports, health and fitness, and any other industry.

Then, create something that your people really really need based on the feedback received. And talk to friends, strangers, people in grocery stores, and just get as much feedback as you can. Don't worry about what you are launching, worry about what is happening in that industry as a whole. The reason why you are NOT consistent is because you started creating what YOU wanted and expected everyone to FLOCK towards it. That is not how this works. And then you got tired and then you got weary. And then, you quit. Because of you and your ego trying to force your idea down people's throats. Am I making yes? Please nod in an affirmative manner. I can see you with this book!! (Inserts Laughter as you look around to see if I am really around).

People were already foolishly chasing their dreams before me.

But I added an identity to it and Foolies is a love child of over 10+ years of hearing people talk about their struggles regarding dream chasing and listening to the friends who were doctors and lawyers who wanted to be cupcake designers and radio personalities. This is me sifting through thousands of comments on IG, YOUTUBE, Twitter, and searching hashtags seeing what people were really asking about. What pain were they experiencing and how can I provide them with a place where they can call home. Then, I created Foolies. Yeah, the name was thought of on its own, but when I got down to the heart of what I wanted to do that is the exercise I implemented. So I don't need to fight to be consistent. Just like you don't need to fight to breathe in fresh air or eat food. It is part of you. Do you want to be consistent? Don't just think about branding. Think about how you can make what you are doing apart of your Deoxyribonucleic acid (DNA for the Homies ;-). Hey, I just used my Sports Medicine degree right there! BOOM! College was a success! Okay...Moving on...After you do the top part of what was mentioned then THIS stuff below just adds on to growing the brand and getting people RIGHT back to your email list :-). Oh, one more thing: Want to make money? Solve problems. And if you want to make millions work on impacting a million people first. I am not the originator of that quote. I have heard key people in the business space or thought leader space that I imagine like Paul C. Brunson and Jason Silva say this. Two more virtual mentors to add to the list amongst many.

Disclaimer: What I will share with you next is things that have worked for me. Take the meat and leave the potatoes or veggies or whatever part of the meal you don't like. There are always some gems and there are some things that won't work for you, but I needed to share my story. I am doing my absolute best as I give you every line and every sentence of this book.

I am a huge wrestling fan. This is all thanks to my pops. And even though our past hasn't been the best I love him to death and love him for getting me hooked on this stuff. Now, I am not talking about UFC or MMA per se (although I did wrestle in college and practiced Muay Thai and Brazilian Jiu-Jitsu for a bit) or traditional Greco style wrestling. I am talking WWE (or what you may remember it as WWF). The one thing about the WWE brand that I admire is that they just keep going. While it may not be interesting for everyone they keep going. They keep evolving. They keep adding to the formula and remixing everything that they do. They have hit their 1000th episode of Smackdown, Have more than 25 years of Monday Night Raw under their belt and the brand has been going on for about 40 years. That is really not a long time. Maybe even that gives you hope. Now their biggest thing is that they also understand who their audience is. They are not worrying about who don't like their brand. They focus on the people that do.

Often times, my inspiration comes from brands around me. Even when people think brands have failed and give up on them I watch them just to see what will happen next. The story always gets greater when people give up on you. At least that is how I've always felt.

I remember when Netflix was "failing." I literally said, "NETFLIX IS ABOUT TO RISE LIKE A PHOENIX" after seeing an article about the demise of the brand and how they would never work. That company is making more money now than it could ever imagine.

Tough times sometimes bring out the best in people. It may push you to be the most innovative you have ever been. In the face of fear, you will find yourself finding more willpower than when everything is going well and you are making tons of money. Then you see why you are REALLY doing what you do. Foolies got to a point where we weren't making any sales.

People would only sit around waiting for discounts or when we did sales. But this was my fault. I only posted and shared things that said "BUY BUY BUY." While of course, you need to make money my balance was off. I wasn't being consistent with the heart of what the brand truly stood for. One day I somehow ended up to a free conference about digital marketing and branding and got the best lesson I could ever receive. Get your pens/highlighters/notes app out:

80% of the content you create/share/discuss/post should be for your fans/audience/friends. 20% is you promoting your business.

Miss out on that and you lose out greatly. This formula has allowed me to stay with this thing for the last 7+ years (and will push me to go another 7+). I really wish I could remember the name of the lady who told me that. At this point (maybe 2012-2013) I had heard tons of advice. But that 80/20 concept has helped me the most and it was very different from a lot of the other things I was reading at the time.

Quick interruption...

Here's Your Mission: For the next 3 days. Only 3. Share something positive to your timeline. A news story. A positive video. Or even something that is funny. A meme, or someone being silly or foolish. This sounds cheesy but you may just brighten someone's day. They may be having a tough day at work and your meme even if it's dark and sarcastic could at least help them out. I follow a young lady who shares memes all day. I saw someone say on her status once, "Thanks so much. You don't know how you get me through my day." We all can play our part. And you can do that with zero dollars in your pocket.

Now back to it.

So here are some thangs (Yes, thangs) that I wasn't doing:

I wasn't building an email list (I will keep winking at this).

I wasn't giving them a day of the week to connect with me. Foolies Fridays is very strategic. Every single day of the week if you miss everything from me you know you will get something on a Friday. What will your day of the week thing be? Manic Mondays? Turn Up Tuesdays? These sound like night club promotions, but there is a reason why they do what they do and why they are (not all, but a lot) successful. Creating a day of the week to consume content on me should have happened from the beginning. The goal is to get this to the point where I can do videos daily. But I too, still wrestle with imposter syndrome and thinking about things like "Who cares what I am doing?" People care. Don't be like me and be fighting with yourself for years. You can change it all tomorrow morning while using your smartphone.

I wasn't (in the beginning) asking people nor was I listening to what they needed. I should have been finding the pain points sooner and building a brand around what they needed. I wasn't upholding the mission to inspire people to foolishly live out their dreams.

I mean I was doing this, but it wasn't as consistent as I would have liked. But as I said that 80/20 advice changed it all. I realize that I didn't need to be the creator of all the things I shared. I needed to be the curator of it all. Anything positive goes through me. Anything uplifting the black culture goes through me. Anything empowering the masses and shining a light on their dreams it goes through me. I became the PLUG for all things positive and uplifting. It was easy to be consistent when I became the curator and stopped trying to create it all myself. I ate, slept, and breathed motivational/aspirational/and spiritual content.

More things I did (and that I continue to do):

I watch plenty of sermons. TD Jakes, Steven Furtick, and a strong list of others who are just great orators. I probably became the self-help book guru for a minute. Tony Robbins, John C. Maxwell, Seth Godin, and the list continues. I wanted to make sure my cup was running over as I gave to the masses. So every investment in myself I would end up giving it all away to the people around me. As I learned something, I gave. Learned a little more, I gave. Then I thought about well, why don't I share my thoughts and feelings and encouragement with the youth? Me simply having a college degree could inspire them to do something great. So I would start reaching out to teachers that I knew who were working at high schools and middle schools and ask to come in and speak. I would try to get opportunities to go in on special days where the school may be looking for professionals. TEACH IN was a big one. The things I would share on my social media platforms I gave it a name as well: Positive Propaganda. I wanted to create a different narrative around black and brown people. I didn't want to only see that we were thugs, or getting into fights. So I then searched for the positivity within my community. Became the champion of all things uplifting. After some time, I could develop certain catchphrases and concepts behind it.

#FooliesApproved came about when I figured this was me cosigning on a product and saying that it was something positive, inspiring, uplifting, and this would also be a sign of someone saying "Wow, that was foolish of them to try but they pulled it off."

I would then start creating content once or twice a week until I was able to start creating things once or twice a day. Once again, the beauty of what I am sharing with you is that you don't have to start from scratch. You can easily hire a photographer. Go out and shoot on some dope locations in your city. Take the pics, drop texts, or

filters, or whatever resonates with you. You can use apps like Snapseed and Canva to do some amazing things as well. Once again, Mailchimp is my baby. And it is free. Use it. Build that email list. Keep your audience informed. Give them sneak peeks at products. Hook them up. Give them a reason to be on that VIP list.

Now, we had a season where Foolies just wasn't doing anything. Why am I mentioning this again? Because it wasn't just one time. It was several times. Several seasons. Several occasions.

Fell into another creative ditch.

Got all self-conscious in what I was putting out.

This caused me to not want to promote the brand as much.

Another dry spell was in place.

This made me sit down with my COO and say, "Hey, what are we going to do if we are not dropping photos of t-shirts anymore." And I think my response after going back and forth was that I need to inspire people daily or weekly. Nothing more nothing less. The pro tip here would be: Don't do it (run a business, start a youtube page, etc) with any intentions or concepts behind it. Just do it because you never know who needs you." That may not be the most business-y advice I could give you. But I did that in the beginning. Now, this is just letting you inside of my mind and my heart.

So about 4 years ago, we started posting a lot more encouragement. If not every day then it was at least weekly. Then, I started doing my Friday video series, Foolies Fridays. Now, I tried to do a Foolies vlog thing years ago, but I quit and gave up. I've been blogging since the summer of 2007 on and off. But once again, I didn't stay consistent. Had a website called iAmThatGreat (the capital letters stood for Alexander The Great), but you know the routine with that. Started, and eventually stopped. You see I write this book to make sure you

as the reader know that 1. You can do this too. I am merely a Clark Kent, A Peter Parker. But the will and determination deep within will make you greater than I could ever be, And 2. This is my plea to you out there wherever you are. If you are traveling on a plane, lonely and in your bedroom, or living in a mansion on 200+ acres with a Tesla in the front. FIND THAT WHY AND KEEP YOUR LASER FOCUS ON THAT VERY WHY! This is what recharged me and got me to start creating content every single day. It became my fix. It became my high. Who else could I impact? Who else can I touch? How can I keep

my eyes more open and aware so that I could be touched as well? Because of course, it is not just about me impacting you. The more I feel the impact from the game changers around me the more I can continue to impact others. A few things I want you to do especially with Social Media going forward:

1. This is a see first tab. This is what you see when you visit someone's business page on Facebook. Go to each and every page that inspires you and uplifts you and hit the see first feature. This means that you will see the posts from this page before you see everything else. Go hit that Foolies Clothing page on Facebook and start with us.

Why am I instructing you to do this? Well, the first thing you start seeing when you login or open up that Facebook app needs to change. This is how you restructure your mind to the things that are possible. This is why I don't see as much negativity on my page. Plus, anyone who is being negative I will usually unfollow or hide for 30 days. That is a feature as well which I am sure you all know.

Now here is another friendly competition thing I do. The people who I put on see first anytime I see them post I say to myself "Nemo, what kind of content can you create?" "Nemo, have you been working on editing that 5-minute video to a 30-second video?" "Nemo, can you drop anything? Someone needs you!" I use that as fuel and create content. That is another way I stay consistent.

How do I, Sir Nemo, Prince of the Sea, Master of the rhymes, Slayer of Motivation, stay consistent:

I know why I am doing this and who I am doing this for.

I compete in a friendly way with the people around me.

People need to see and understand what I am doing multiple times in multiple platforms. How will I get my name out there and my business out there if I don't make what I stand for and what the company stands for evident? That is the importance of the 80/20. The 80 percent of things I share I merely put my #FooliesApproved stamp on it. It is already positive and uplifting. It allows people to understand the content I want to be shared with me. Now, people are always tagging me and putting me in uplifting conversations and sending me things.

I read and consume a lot of things that push me to create. Ideas and feelings and emotions that align with mines and some that even challenge my normal train of thought.

Follow brands that are doing it well and figure out how you can emulate the concept for your brand. You can be inspired without copying. You can do things similar but still make it your own at the same time.

Either way, curate the social life/real life that you want for the career you want to get into or the lifestyle you want to live. So for me as I think I have mentioned (as I now get a little more specific) it's Sermons from Steven Furtick and Elevation Church, It's uplifting videos from Tom Bilyeu and all the dope people who he has interviewed with Impact Theory, Seth Godin Books, and content that Will Smith is creating. And what he is doing right now is absolutely bananas and I am learning a lot from him. <u>Go look up the video he did when he told his brother in law about breaking into the movie business</u>. And you can definitely add the <u>Roommates Podcast</u> to the list. Those young boys are doing their thing. Hopefully, they don't stop the grind. A lot of positive stuff just floating around for us to consume. Let that feed you and inspire you to greater things.

I think that's all I got for now....(Insert Michael Jackson's Thriller Ending Laugh)

Oh, one more thing at the end of every single day just ask yourself: What Good Have I done for the World Today? That also helps me too. Not just for what I post and create online but for the people I interact with when the cameras aren't blazing.

Ohhhh...One more thing.

How did I get featured in the Gary Vee book? Consistency worked in a different way for me on this one. At the time I was watching Gary Vee's content a lot. Gary Vaynerchuck for those who don't know the full name of who I am talking about. He's a really dope entrepreneur that builds businesses, buys businesses, and talks a lot on marketing and branding. You may like him, you may not. Alright, back to the story…

So I was consistently watching his videos. He has two aspects to his show: Ask Gary Vee Show and The Daily Vee. Most people will consume The Daily Vee because it is more like a blog about his life and what he does and his meetings etc.

For some reason, I just consumed both, but I leaned more towards the Ask Gary Vee show. So I remember one day it was at the end of a RAAANNNDDOOOOMMM episode I think of either or show and he was doing a "call" of sorts. He said in the video (mildly paraphrasing) "If you read my book called "Crush It" and had any impact in your life send me an email. And maybe you will get chosen to be in the new book." I think they were featuring 49 people in the book.

Now, I've sent Gary emails in the past, no response.

Tried to be on the Ask Gary Vee Show, got a slight response. I got as far as a phone call with some of his team but I wasn't the best fit I imagine so nothing went forward.

That should have made me say "Forget Gary, and his team, I don't need him." It should have…But, why get all bent out of shape. I just figured the moment or situation was a "NOT YET" kinda deal.

So when I saw that call for anyone who has read his book I was like OH SNAP, this may be my shot. Here is the exact email I sent:

Peep that date in the top corner!! December 2016. Yep! No worries on my end. Just gonna keep doing my thing. I don't even remember when I got the response back, but my mind was blown. Now, let's fast forward through time. I talk to Gary's team. They wanted to talk to me more so they could gather some more info from me before they would decide to put me in the book. We had to set a date. Look at God right quick. The young lady on Gary's team asked me if JUNE 28TH WAS A GOOD DATE FOR OUR PHONE CALL/MEETING? Do you all know that June 28th is my bday?!?!? I said nothing about that and just was like, "Yep, that will be great. Talk to you then."

Now, this was also the year when the magic was happening and for my 30th bday, I was going to New Orleans for EssenceFest. Now, I said this may be a year or two before my 30th that I am going to find a way there. Then God blessed me again and one of my best friends bought me a ticket. Boom. But, I still had no money per se for the actual trip itself. But hey, one part down. Another part to go. Alright, so I think the morning before my flight I did what I thought was a really big interview. It was told to me that it was gonna debut on SlingTV and all kinds of cool stuff. I am not sure what happened, but I never saw that interview. I got a subscription for a week or so to see if I would catch it and no go. Plus, none of my friends really had sling so it was really me hoping to maybe record or snap screenshots and tell my friends. But, I wasn't gonna let that de-motivate me either. I've been working on Foolies for a long time.

I have had a lot of promises made to me. I have sent my clothing to hundreds of celebs, influencers, big names, small names etc. I have DM'd hundreds of people about my brand. I have emailed hundreds of people about what I am doing. I have been a vendor. I have kissed babies. I have been active on social (media). I have found creative ways to promote. I have built value. I don't ask for much. But in this moment, I was like please let this Gary opportunity come through, please.

So boom, I'm in New Orleans. Just hopped out of an Uber with a really nice lady. She told me her son was into business and so I told her about a few books and threw Crush It in there as well. No special reason other than because it helped me. Hopped out the Uber and walked into a hostel. I thought I was going to have to stay there because I didn't know what I was about to do. I just showed up in New Orleans. No plans. No nothing. I was going to figure it out. One of the things I do on my bday is I ask for a $1. I figured since I was going to New Orleans whatever my friends gave me I would use that to try to survive these next days on the trip. I get a phone call and in my head I am thinking I need to be genuine, but still pour my heart out with this call. I think me and a young lady from Gary's team spoke for an hour and change. Telling her everything from Foolies starting out as just an idea. And how I used to wrap. Then talking about the canned messages with the t-shirts inside and the personal handwritten letter. I mentioned how my friends funded my trip to New Orleans and how this shirt with these dope black women on it changed my life. I was merely highlighting them because they deserved it but it turned into so much more. I felt good after the call, but once again, I had been made promises before in life and things didn't come through, so I just kept my cool and I enjoyed my time in New Orleans.

Might I add and just say EssenceFEST was absolutely amazing. And the thing is, I didn't do all the party stuff. I just went to some of the events that surrounded business and marketing. They had a few seminars. A young lady I met at the event hooked me up with a pass, so I could get in to the business stuff. A frat brother let me crash on the couch. The couple dollars I had helped me survive for the weekend. That was also when I had my new camera the Sony A6000 and I was parading around like I was an official photographer. It did help somewhat. I was still trying to provide value for people while being there the entire time. So as guest speakers were doing their thing I would capture photos of them and tag them on Twitter. It's not about me...Never has...Never will....Any event I couldn't really get to I would just ask and plead a little bit and since it was my 30th I got to pull that card a few times. Hey, gotta do what you gotta do. I wanted to make moves. So that is what mattered most to me. Not my stupid pride. And it was just so melanated. So amazing. So much love. So many dope black celebs. So many black-owned businesses. I was literally in heaven. Complimenting practically anyone I ran into. Nice hair, nice bag, love your this...love your that...I snapped more photos. And learned as much as I could. Got to hear amazing people like Issa Rae speak, Mara Brock Akil, Holly Robinson Pete, Jessica O. Matthews, Tiffany "The Budgetnista" and the list goes on and on. I couldn't help while being there just hoping and praying that one day I will get to be on these stages. That one day I would get to be next to these amazing individuals. That one day I would have them coming up to me at the end of an event hoping to connect with me. That was on my mind the entire time while being there. I knew when I got home that my consistency would have to ramp up even more.

A few weeks before Gary's release date my answer as to if I made it in the book was answered. This guy messaged me and said he loved my section in the book. Gary gave him an early copy and he was happy he skimmed across my section from pages 53-58. I jumped for joy. I didn't cry for once, but man, I was relieved. Then January 30th, 2018 came and I ran to Barnes and Noble's to cop me the book and to tell my friends the announcement.

Yeah, consistency did all of this. Me consistently pounding away at the dream no matter the outcome or the storyline. The many prayers and many tears did all of this as well. I am not where I want to be just yet, but I am being used to make an impact on a couple more hundred people. I will take that for now as I still push towards bigger and better things.

Yo Yo!! Has this been helpful? Make sure you find me on IG and chat real quick: @Foolies. Show me some love. Give a shout out. Create an Instastory and let people know that you are reading the Foolies Approved book right now!!

Here's Your Mission:

Find 3-5 friends who wouldn't mind being in a chat/email thread with you. State the purpose of the group: Inspiration, Money Tips, Working out etc. This could be a small group but could be something that has a profound impact on your life or career. All these apps we have out there: GroupMe, Slack, Gmail, etc. Pick one and go to town.

Want to start your podcast show today with ZERO dollars and with your cell phone? There's an app called Anchor. It's a podcast app. It's free. You can record your episodes right from your home in your PJs. Talk about whatever you want. Your favorite sports, music, or if you have a positive message to promote then do that too. Don't see the positive news about Black America? Use your own platform to get it out there. Never seeing enough positive messages on display? Google positive news topics and then talk about them on your podcast show that cost you nothing to start. You are already paying for that thousand dollar IPhone or Samsung device. You might as well use it for good.

CHAPTER:-6

THE NEMO NETWORKING GUIDE

Waves hands from side to side

When I say net yall say work

Net

Work

Net

Work

When I say net

Now yall say worth

Net

Worth

Net

Worth

Build up ya network

Then grow ya net worth

Build up ya network

Then grow ya network!!

Check me out right…

The most unlikely way for you to learn how to network starts with this lesson. First, l lost my mom to breast cancer, right? But then I had to go live with my pops. We stayed with his fiancé at the time and her family in Liberty City. Now if you don't know liberty city just think of that place in your town that you probably don't wanna go jogging around when the streetlights come on. And that was if they even came on. I used to catch this bus thing called the jitney. With the jitney it would ride on a specific route all around the city of Miami. In order for the driver to know when you wanted to stop you had to yell "BUS STOP!" If I didn't

yell out bus stop I would potentially miss my stop. I miss my stop, I miss school. Can't miss school. Everything I was doing was for the moms at this point. I stepped my game up drastically. Literally went from D's and F's in conduct and C's in classes to As and Bs. I hate that losing her had to teach me the valuable lessons she was trying to instill in me before. And even my mom's kindness I take with me in a room while meeting and connecting with people. I even imagine that people are my old friends from back in the day. Creating that energy helps a lot.

And I think I mentioned that my dad's fiancé later left him and took his money, right? If I didn't or you forgot...then just know that was something that happened. After that, me and my dad went to go live with a friend of the family. At first, I thought it was supposed to be for a little while until we got on our feet. That little while turned into a few years and a majority of my high school career. I looked up to this lady as my Aunt. In this household we had about 10+ kids, including me and my pops. Then, since it was such a big family of course you had to think about the cousins, friends, and friends of friends that would come visit on vacations, holidays, during the summertime the works.

So wait Nemo, I thought this chapter was about networking. It is fam, just pump your breaks. You don't see what is happening here do you?

What do you think I had to do when I moved in with my dad's fiancé and their family or my pseudo Aunt's family? I had to introduce myself. Get to know complete strangers. Create bonds. Build friendships. But, living in someone else's home wasn't always fun. The kids who didn't understand that I lost my mom and was going through a tough time would say things like "This my mama house, why you here?" Or "Why you using my mama stuff?" or "Why are you even here can't you and your daddy find somewhere else to go?" And of course, we were kids and they didn't know if their words hurt me or not but it did. The toughest part was feeling like I didn't truly belong. While living with my aunt there were always moments to take the big family photo. I wasn't always in it. With some people in the house I felt I was like a brother, others I felt like I was just a "distant cousin" and others understood that I was there because I fell on tough times. Whether this was communicated or not this was just how I felt. Eventually, my dad would leave me at my aunt's place and that was an interesting season as well. There were times where I truly felt alone. And there wasn't always clarity if I would have a place to live or not. So imagine what that must have felt like while I was trying to hold it down in high school? I am sure the thought dawned on the family to put me out or to find my dad wherever he was and have me live with him, but it risked me not having a place to go to school. My dad didn't necessarily care about what happened to me. He thought I was good. He peaced out and did his thing. The toughest parts were knowing he was secretly planning to leave and me worrying what was about to happen to me. I got used to disappointment. It wouldn't be the first time. When I was younger, and my mom and dad were separated he would promise to pick me up on the weekends. I remember we had a large glass window that we could see anyone who pulled up to the driveway. I had a purple metallic bag that I would pack with my toys and other things full of excitement. My mom knew he wasn't coming. I would sit there like a puppy waiting for his owner to arrive. Filled with hope that he would come. Once again, I wasn't a novice to my dad and his disappointment. So, him leaving me in this situation wasn't shocking.

But wait...Nemo, what does this have to do with networking?

These moments taught me to treat everyone like they are important. This taught me to stay true to my word and to never make promises that I know I wasn't planning to keep.

When I network I value every single person in the room. I even say, "what up" and show love to housekeeping, secretaries, and the people who run the sound and the video technology (for example at a conference or live event). I hated the times where I felt alone, or no one really liked me or didn't care for me to be around. So now when I am out and about networking I remember and go and shake another hand. Show them the genuine love I wanted more of. Now this is tough because I don't want to paint the picture that the people who raised me or that I had to live with didn't care about me. But, it really taught me to step my game up. Being in a house of 10+ people is a constant networking session. Constantly building relationships. Constantly finding a new crew to connect with. It was a lot of listening to moments where brothers and sisters were fighting. A lot of moments of seeing what would happen when you were pushed or provoked to the limit. I gotten into my share of fights like real brothers and sisters did and there were a lot of moments of laughs and bonds. Either way, this made me more comfortable when I sat down with randoms. I didn't fear being in new rooms or environments since I always was moving and

bouncing from place to place. It allowed me to adapt as needed. It taught me in some cases how to detach when relationships were done and it was time to move on. When you are in a household when everyone is cracking jokes and picking on everyone it made my skin tougher so that much didn't faze me when I got into the real world. The same energy would easily transfer to my college days.

But when I got to college that is where I really felt that emptiness...

The first family I would develop would be with the infamous FRESHman Crew. For those who didn't go to school with me, this was a crew me and some friends formed during our UF days. It started during our freshman year of college and continued on even til this day. Upperclassman thought they were so smart. They would hear us chanting, we not we freshman we FRESH man...and say, "What are you gonna do when you become sophomores..." We would be like "ummm...it still works. Next year we won't be freshman but we still fresh...maaaann!!" So there's some context for those who don't know me and that world...

Now, let others tell you the story it may be different...But, I lowkey created the name of the crew. I don't say it in a really bragging kind of way...but, I am just throwing it out there in love. We were in one of the homies dorms and we were listening to Jay Z and that is when he dropped the infamous line "I'm not a businessman, I'm a business man..." And the thought came to me... "We not freshman....We FRESH MAN!" and it was all in sync and we all agreed it was tight. So essentially, it was a collective thought. Maybe not even me per se, but yeah haha.

I did say I would be bragging lightly right? Okay, cool.

But that group of dudes/brothers taught me a lot. They taught me confidence. They taught me how to not take myself so seriously. There were highs and lows and I wasn't always around, but they were still the first group I truly connected with. With a crew of 10 or 12 guys and girls running around UF screaming at parties and events "WE NOT FRESHMAN...WE FRESH MAN...AYE!!" (That was the era of Juelz Santana so I imagined that is where that got adopted.) But, we were all kids from all around the country with a common goal to change the UF game by any means necessary. From Miami to Lauderdale, to DUUUUVAAALLLL, from west coast to east coast...we were truly a mashup of a lot of different personalities and Carribean backgrounds as well.

We even created chapters of this freshman crew at other schools like FSU, UCF (or at least we tried) and a few other places around the country.

But what does this have to do with networking?

When you are around a dope group of people it will naturally push you to come out of your shell. You need people around you who will motivate you and uplift you. That is what the crew did for me. Even if they weren't deliberately doing that it helped me out a great deal.

The next lesson would come from Greek life.

Now mind you, as a Jamaican America I had no flipping clue what Greek life was. Who were these guys yelling and screaming and doing all these weird hand signs and gestures? Is this a gang? This was 2005. I just turned 18. The next year I would find myself doing the same thing as a brother of Alpha Phi Alpha. I was the

Deuce Club #2, Negotiator, Fall 06, Theta Sigma! Thank God I ran into these group of brothers because they taught me things like how to tie a tie, how to truly be professional, the importance of giving back to my community and so much about brotherhood and family that I had never gotten in my life...If it wasn't for one brother, in particular, Will Atkins who was such a dope role model at UF I would have never been inspired to be part of the organization. I didn't necessarily have all the confidence, so I made sure I got active and involved with people who did. I wasn't always good at networking, but I put myself around people who had it down pat. After joining the frat I was pushed to put on events, shows, perform in front of large crowds, and a whole lot of public speaking.

And even before that I had my season with a dance troupe. Apocalypse Dance Troupe. We were a spin off of the FAMU Strikers so I did/we did a lot of booty shaking in my day and hip hop dancing. Wasn't always the best dancer, but I did what I could and I was the king of doing handstands and backflipping. Another organization that I had to be bold and put myself out there in order to be successful.

And remember that Jitney I had to catch? If I didn't get bold and yell out bus stop I would have missed my stop. A lot of yall missing yall stops or spots in the game because you not putting yourself out there and/or speaking up. I can't help your mission if I don't even know you to know you have a mission worth helping.

Put yourself in the position to be great. I wanted to be amongst the legends. So I put myself in positions to connect with them. That was how I networked. That is how I consistently came out of my shell.

And having the name Nemo helped as well. How did I get the nickname you ask? Well, I guess it's finally time I shared that as well...

But before we do that...Here's your mission:

What two or three people can you connect who may need to know each other? They may all be photographers, creatives, lawyers and doctors. They may need to know each other. They may have ideas that are great but connecting them would be the thing they need to take off. Is there an event that you can share that matches your friends interest? Then share it. Look it up. Hop on Eventbrite and find something. It may be the one thing your friend needed so they can change the world. Oh, you don't have to be the one that does the world shaping. You can easily be the middleman to someone else's greatness.

Also, what's your nickname? Don't go by your real name for a change. Share a family nickname with someone next time you meet. Me being "Nemo" has taught many people to not take themselves so seriously and has helped me make greater bonds with people. Greater bonds equal deeper friendships. More enriching friendships can be the fuel to help you change the world. My personal opinion. But, even just a laugh and a story could go a long way. And guess how much you had to pay for that? Zero.

Want to go a little further? You can start a Facebook group for free. Find all the experts on whatever topic of your interest (Comics, Netflix, Sports, etc) in your city through Facebook, IG, and/or by word of mouth and just add them to a Facebook group. Create some posting rules and guidelines and make your own community. Guess how much you will have to pay for that? You guessed right. ZERO-Ninety-Nine.

DJ...Next track...

CHAPTER:-7

HOW TO BECOME INTERNET FAMOUS

Well there is a real story and a fake real story. The fake real story goes...I was wearing a Nemo backpack at my orientation when I went to THE Great University of Florida. At some point in my session this orientation leader asked me, "Yo, why the Nemo backpack?"

In my head I'm like oh crap...

I can't tell this dude that I wore it so that girls could say awww that's cute and then I could put my mack down.

So I needed to come up with something clever and it puts me in a good light...but not a complete horseradish of a lie...

So here's what I said...

it was so good...

Being the freestyle king that I am I said:

"You know Nemo encompasses my childlike innocence and no matter how old I get I will have that youthfulness within me. Also, I would love to work for the Pixar team one day and be part of their animation team so this is me paying homage to the company as a whole so that is why I wear the bag."

Can you say mic drop?!?!! Ohhhhhh, he wasn't ready!!!!!!

First off, I didn't even remember if Nemo was even made by Pixar lol. Secondly, I did want to become an animator but got discouraged from that dream early. Also, was that not a smooth cover up?

Now, the real story...

I was working for a phone fundraising company called Repdials my freshman year. And that crew I told you about? Invited me to a freestyle battle after work. Now mind you, I was told to just show up because everyone was gonna be there and so I did. So I rush out of work and try to get to this really cool coffee club type place on campus called the Orange and Brew. I get there and I think it was Swain that said "Nemo, we put you on the list." Now I would love to tell you that I was super excited and just ready to go but my heart fell into my stomach like Will Smith jumping out of that helicopter on his 50th birthday and then being yanked back up into my chest because now I have to perform, and I never said I wanted to be in this battle.

So it's game time. We flip a coin. Me and some random guy that I don't remember. I call tailed and it's heads. So my heart starts pounding harder and harder cause I'm like crap man there's an advantage I would get to going last because I can flip everything they're saying against them.

I had to think about this quickly. If I am gonna rap against someone tonight they are gonna use the whole Nemo thing against me. I literally thought about B rabbit in 8 mile and I said, I have to diss myself before my opponent can.

But I found a way to twist this moment to my favor. So with my backward cap on that said Nemo on it and my baggy white tee and Girbaud Jeans gets on the mic and says the next choice of words...

Now before I tell you I just ask for this to be a nonjudgment zone. You can't post about this unless it's like a private message or something...

You know what? I ain't gon tell y'all because yall petty. And this would be all over the place. But whatever...

So I said to the dude I know this gon make you upset the reason why they call me Nemo is because I keep ya girl wet...

Now, I may have used another name or word for "girl" so use your imagination. And the crowd went bananas!!

Ohhhhhh he keep ya "girl" wet!! Ohhhhhh!!! Mind you, I'm 18. Young and dumb. It just was me having a good time. But every time people saw me with the backpack on they remembered me. Everywhere I went between orientation and after that event, NEMO stuck. Plus, the fact that I carried the backpack everywhere helped for memory sake. The funny part was that there were sometimes where I didn't wear the backpack and people were like "Hey, have we met?" And then I was like remember me? Nemo? With the bookbag? "Ohhhhh, Nemo!! Where yo bag at?"

See, before you become internet famous you need to become

local famous, or campus famous. Be famous or be super dope in your own little quadrant before you end up being famous for the world to see. Before my work got shared by Luvvie (If you don't know here then you need to know her) my work was being shared by my friends, colleagues, and their friends would see it and then say "Hey, since you cosigned on that Aquafinaisha I am going to watch it as well." Word of mouth is powerful. That is how things get around the best. And I know something is powerful if I don't tell you to share and you still share. But, I do understand that I do need to at least suggest to share things that I post and create to at least plant that seed. Sometimes people don't know how they can support until you tell them.

Another funny part to the Nemo story is that I almost bought a STITCH book bag instead of the Nemo. See, the bookbag thing was just something we did back in high school. Yes, from Lilo and Stitch. I always think about what would my line be in the freestyle battle if I was called Stitch versus Nemo? I am sure I could have finessed something. But yeah, I almost bought a stitch bag. But, I figured Nemo would be a little more universal.

Also, Nemo broke a lot of barriers. I was a kid from the hood, fitted caps, baggie jeans, Diadora's and Air Forces on with Golds in my mouth and a chain/pendant of my mom dangling around my neck. If you didn't understand that style or feel of culture you may have not wanted to talk to me. Just being real. But people seeing the Nemo book bag made them say, "Hey, I love Nemo! Just keep swimming. Just keep swimming."

Now here is another secret: I had never seen the movie until like my sophomore or junior year of college. I saw bits and pieces but never went to theatres to see it. Yes, I was wearing the bag and being real fraudulent out here. But, I caught on to the different punchlines and references and would be able to adapt with the convos

people were throwing at me. But here is how God is very interesting...So my friend who I will call Pinky (because that's the nickname I gave her back in college. She called me Brain. Yes, like the 90s tv show) said to me one day the strangest thing. She said "Nemo, do you call yourself that because Nemo didn't have a mom either?" I think I was drinking water and spit it up a little bit and was like what? Now, I had been able to keep up with a lot of references and that was one I didn't know. Then, I finally went back and watched the movie and I was like woooooooww. Me and this character weren't too far off of each other. To an extent of course. But, it was very interesting nonetheless.

Ultimately, that bag and that name created a connection. You want to be internet famous? How are you connecting to your audience? How are you serving them? Are you listening to what they want and creating content around that?

When I created the legendary Be Strong Like Regina Tee I was catching a moment RIGHT after Viola Davis had won her first Emmy. Regina King had also won her Emmy that day as well. I didn't watch the awards show. I woke up at about 5 / 6 am in the morning and saw the clips of those two women and I literally balled/cried. I cried and said these words… "God, these women just want their shot. They just want to be heard and they want to be put on the same playing field as their counterparts." I still remember hearing the words "This is the first Emmy win and nomination for Viola Davis…" being read by the commentator. My heart was full. I was so packed with emotion and I didn't know what to do. I started making the graphic right after I watched those two clips...I got on CANVA and wrote this out…

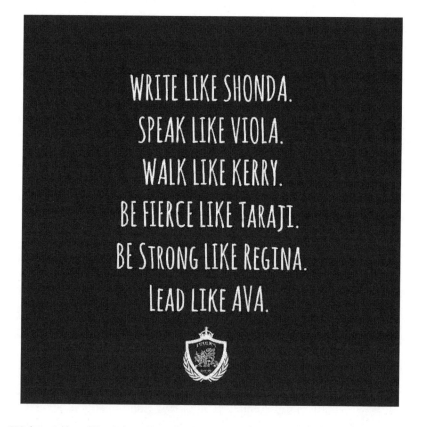

Write Like Shonda, Speak Like Viola, Walk like Kerry, Be Fierce Like Taraji, Be Strong like Regina, Lead like Ava. See something weird about this? Well, This wasn't how the shirt came out. This was dropped on September 21st, 2015. The morning after the Emmys. After all the controversy and the issues. All I did was hop on my platform and say hey, why not give people flowers while they can still smell them? I posted this at like 9:13 am and went to work. Mind you...Before I dropped this a few things happened 1. I texted this to Alisa Valentin (college homie and amazing young lady) and said what do you think about this graphic? 2. I was talking to my friend Lanae that morning. I was asking her what should I write? And does this even sound good? 3. My homegirl Cita, I sent this to her and was like what do you think. She said it's dope and asked if I was going to make this into a shirt. I said nah, I don't wanna do this for no shirt purposes. I just want to uplift these women and that's it. She insisted, Make it into a shirt. I still, with my stubborn behind, said nah.

Before I continue...When black women tell you to do something, you do it. Because they just got something in the soul and their gut that just be knowing.

Alisa responded with, "I needed that today." Or "I needed that this morning." Something of that nature. Now Alisa is a UF grad and killing the game of course and she went to an HBCU so I was like she hella woke and if she approves of this shirt I am still in the game.

For all my homies, that is also a quick message. Who gives you the green light on some of your concepts before you drop them?

Everything may not be ready to hit the world just yet. And of course, take their thoughts with a grain of salt. But, I knew she would be a perfect person to give me a green light on if something should make it to the public. Especially, something that was so encompassing of dope black women. She on her PhD flow as well yall! My friends are so amazing...Okay...Now back to the message...

Now, after I made that post I got into my day of working, but something was off. The entire my morning my phone kept buzzing. Bzzz Bzzz Bzzz Bzzz. I'm like what the flip is going on. My thought process was that I must have gotten thrown in some lame group chat message on FB and now people promoting to me. But, that wasn't the case.

I checked my FB and the image that I posted had like 50 likes and 20-30 something shares. I was like oh, that's interesting. Must be my homies who really liked it. But then I saw a bunch of comments and figured let me say something as well because people were saying "hey, you missed a person." or hey, "this is dope and so powerful..." The comments were great but one comment shook me. It came from Luvvie Ajayi. Someone made a comment and then Luvvie (who also shared the graphic) was like "Hey Alex, is this your graphic?" Me knowing that this is one of the DOPEST, the FLYEST, and the COOLEST (at least to me) content creators on the web like a little kid I was like "Yeah, it's me!" I think she told me to message her and that is when it all went down.

Mind you, I am at work. Full-time job swaggin' I wasn't just home, chilling, living my best Entrepreneur life. I was trying to pay bills while I grow this baby at the same time.

Luckily my COO, Kimberly was able to finish up the Convo with Luvvie and get the shirt up for the masses who was yelling take my money.

If you notice the Tee looked different than the original graphic.

I thought the hype was over until February of 2016. I get an email from the Essence team saying that they would like anywhere between 12-15 shirts for an event they were having called Black Women in Hollywood. The event would have Hollywood's brightest stars out and about. And my shirts were going to be used for an all youth girls' choir.

Mind you, I am knocked out and sleeping on the floor. I had this whole season of wanting to be "grounded," so I started sleeping on the floor because I felt like I was getting soft by being in a bed all the time. I know, I am weird.

But, Kimberly our amazing and dynamic and super awesome (I'm buttering her up because I know I messed up at first) COO called and told me about the email...My response, "We can't do anything about that order, we don't have shirts on us." I wasn't lying. At the time we weren't printing shirts anymore. We stopped because we were losing a lot of money just having inventory on hand. Being a vendor wasn't working for us. And, it just became a hassle to buy hundreds of shirts over and over and guesstimating what the sizes would be and what would be most popular. Even if we looked at the stats someone would always surprise us and mess everything up.

Everything went through Teespring after our first viral moment. Teespring was able to handle hundreds and it could handle up to thousands of orders from what I am imagining.

I sprung up immediately after that call was over. I couldn't believe I had said those words as if this wasn't the biggest moment of my natural born life. Luckily, I had just left the old company I was printing with because I didn't feel valued to a different company that goes by the name of Metropolis here in Orlando. I called them the next morning and said hey, I need

12-15 tees, but, I need you to send them off to Hollywood once you are done. They worked with me because normally they didn't do orders that low. Usually, printing bulk means 30+, 50+. I hit up my best friends DC and Trina and my fave Tiffuhknee and told them the situation and they kindly gave me some funds to be able to pay for this order that had come up so quickly. Plus, what they gave me plus what I had on me was able to cover overnight shipping as well with some form of tracking on there if I am not mistaken. It's been some time now so--yeah...

Now could you imagine how frantic and nervous I am. Praying, hoping, wishing, and praying that these shirts make it to this Black Women In Hollywood event. Now like a true worry-wart that I am I was like "God, you know what? If it doesn't make it it's all good...I get it...Maybe it wasn't for me..." I just started talking a whole bunch of foolishness. I think I sent the package off either Monday or Tuesday and it got to them either the next day or the next after that. I was going to fuss about it, but I learned that they got it on time and were going to be able to use it for the event. Now, the show (Black Women In Hollywood) is pre-recorded. So that could essentially mean, yeah, the shirts were there but no one will see them as far as national television goes. It was a lot of nervousness the day of the show. I knew it was going to be held the Thursday before the event would air on OWN Network on the following Sunday. My heart grew heavier and heavier. I was hoping someone, anyone, would tweet, or say something in regards to the shirt they were seeing on stage, but it was radio silence the whole show. I saw one post and I was like, I think that is them (the girls) in my shirt but the photo was taken too far back.

I'd given up by this point. Was getting ready to secede and fold and call it a night. "Ping!" A noise via my IG went off. Mind you, my phone never makes noises for IG but today it did. I CHECKED. THE SCREEN LOADED. MOVING SLOW.

I REFRESHED ONCE MORE. THEN I RUBBED MY EYES BECAUSE IT COULDN'T BE TRUE. IT'S A PICTURE WITH THE GIRLS WHO WORE MY SHIRT AND OPRAH WINFREEEEEYYYY!!!!! GET THE FLIP OUTTA HERE!! Now, this was special because Essence is usually pretty on brand. They don't just post things that don't get special treatment and mocked up by the design team, but this was a different moment.

Then, I went berserk. I shared it with my friends. They shared it with their friends. I was stoked.

Also, this was the same afternoon that I lost my keys and wallet in the same day. Yep, even though I am about to share with you one of the dopest stories of my life it also had some human error wrapped in there as well.

Fast-forwarding to the Sunday of the event. I didn't have a

television, but I had Skype. Wait what, Nemo? Hold on. Cut me a break. I hit up my homegirl Sky and told her I needed a huge favor. I wanted to watch black women in Hollywood but through her Skype chat. I didn't have cable and I really wanted to see the show. The whole night goes, and we are seeing nothing. There were good talks and dope tributes, but I was anxious and want to see my tees. 85-90% of the show had passed and I figured it was a wrap. I guess they cut the segment with my tees. I chalked it up to God's plan and just figured if these moments were meant to be it will be. Of course, I was happy about the already snapped photo I got, but seeing it on TV would have just set my heart on fire. The last segment of the show pops up and Sky is giving me comforting words via Skype and all of a sudden we hear singing. I think Sky yelled, I jumped around, and was like "yooooooooooo, those are myyyyyy shirts!!! Yoooooooo!!" Don't remember it all verbatim, but I was excited. But, another failure moment. What you mean Nemo? Well, everyone saw the front of the shirts and not the BACK where the logo was placed. That's when I start kicking myself. I was just like, "How could you loser?" I thanked Sky and we snapped some photos via her tv screen and she sent it over to me.

Later that night I would get another message via IG. BOOM!!!!!! SHONDA RHIMES WITH THE RETWEET!!!! SHONDA RHIMES!!!! OHHHHH MYYY GOOODNESS!!

STRONG like REGINA.
FIERCE like TARAJI.
WRITE like SHONDA.
SHINE like LUPITA.
DELIVER like UZO.
SPEAK like VIOLA.
AGE like ANGELA.
RULE like QUEEN.
WALK like KERRY.
LEAD like AVA.

shondarhimes

Now let's take a pause. What is being internet famous exactly? Being famous on the internet. It doesn't mean I am cool. It doesn't mean I am the man. It doesn't make me better. I am very fortunate that all this stuff has happened, but it really does mean nothing in the grand scheme of things. So what does it mean? Why am I sharing this? Well, I am sharing this because you need to see and hear it from a very normal everyday guy. The same guy who has to go to work and clock in and out just like you.

Now, I will not downplay these events. These events are what lead me here today. These events allow me to speak to you and share with you my rawest and most intimate thoughts. Through the internet, I am able to touch more people than I could ever imagine. So if you want to be internet famous, then please go ahead.

But aim to impact millions of people before you make millions of dollars. Never forget that. Now, back to the story.

So after the retweet, I got all kinds of tweets and retweets and comments thrown at me. My favorites were the ones that said, "Take My Money!" Those are just funny phrases to me and I was so honored. I think I sold a few hundred shirts before the campaign ended. And all of that goes right back into the business. Right back into ads. Right back into buying apparel for photoshoots that I want to do. Or for people who I am watching and thinking has the influence that I would want back for the brand. I have to be super careful who I give apparel to. 1. I am spending my money to do it. I am not always using the funds of the company. 2. I need them to be on brand. Some people will say, "Hey, give me a shirt man, I got you." No you don't "got me" you just cop you a shirt and not play or pose as if you hold some form of impact that you really don't have. That is the other part of being "internet famous." More people reaching out to you asking you for things. And you can't make everyone happy. Or, some people will be upset with you afterward. So as you climb with what you are doing just be careful. Don't get upset. Don't be annoyed. It is just part of the game. I am honored and blessed that people want to reach out to me. I just know I can't respond to it all.

The toughest part is getting suggestions from people about what to do with Foolies. A lot of times it is assumed that I haven't done anything. "Hey, you should send your shirts to (insert celeb name)." "Hey, you need to be a vendor at (insert event)..." It is tough when you are close to the people. You don't tell Nike how to run Nike because you don't see Phil Knight like that. Some of you may have not even known the name of the person that runs the company. And I am sure, people tweet and dm Nike all the time telling them what they should do and who they should be putting their apparel on as well. Once again, be careful. Nike has millions of fans and billions of eyes on them. With greater power (more reach and impact) comes greater responsibility.

And most important, Stay Humble. This stuff happened in 2015/2016. It is 2018 now when I am writing this. That was two years ago. While I can still point towards that win after some time that win won't have the same weight. So I have to keep finding new ideas. New ways to reinvent the wheel. New things to make the company even better than what it was 2 years ago or even 2 days ago. Always improving and growing this wave so it can reach more and impact more people.

Here's your mission: Do you have a friend with a business? Do you see them posting and sharing all the time? Take a second to see what they are doing. If it seems worthy of a share then share it. If you don't want to share it to your main page throw it in your stories on IG or something. If you really like the business then maybe make a purchase. It could go a very long way. You never know. Also, do you have the power to get your friends in higher places? Think about your connections real quick. Maybe you have a cousin that works in the media. Maybe you got a homeboy that is in the music industry that you are super close with. Pass it on to them. Someone randomly sent my graphic and possibly even my contact to Essence and that's how I got featured. We don't have to even say we did it. Just do it. Another Free opportunity to make an impact. And if you do this do it with nothing wanted in return. A lot of people help people with a condition or term applied even if its not being said. Be mindful of setting expectations like that. If you help someone they don't need to do anything for you in return. Just do it off the strength. Got it? Expect nothing in return for helping the next person. Now, if they choose to circle back and help you then cool. But, you will get your blessing a different way. Trust me!

CHAPTER:-8

THE BIG PICTURE

The sound of little heels come down the stairwell. A young girl walks down with the biggest smile on her face dancing with her mom. She makes it to the main floor and it is filled with afros, locs, and women of color walking around. Managers, CFOs, and my COO giving the orders for the day. The little girl stops her mom and says,

Little girl: "I wanna work here one day, Mommy."

Mom: "But honey, you don't even know what we do here."

Little girl: "But, they have hair like me Mommy. A big afro."

Mom: (Smiles and walks out of here).

That is the big picture. That will always be a big picture. That is why I won't be stopping Foolies or any variation of it anytime soon. You see, that little girl in the back of my mind that I have never met drives me. Me thinking about this brand and what it has done for dope melanated women gives me the energy I need to keep this ship afloat.

What else you may ask?

I still replay the night I lost my mom. I didn't even go to the hospital to see her. I was just tired of seeing her in such a state. I remember the last time I saw my mom. Her last words were, "32 cents." By this point the cancer had spread to her brain and there was nothing anyone could do about it. Not me, not God, not anyone. This was the 90s and there weren't too many options on treating cancer. I thought one day that I could become a doctor and find a cure but I never had the heart to stomach blood and guts or anything like that.

I also wasn't good at science. Sciences wrecked me back at UF. But, I was too far in to stop being an Applied Physiology and Kinesiology student. I remember my advisor when she brought me into her office.

Advisor: "Alex, you have failed another core class and you have one more chance else you will be kicked out of the health and human performance college you do know that?"

Me: I know.

It was a short conversation to say the least.

So there went my mindset for thinking I could do anything in that space. Kinda haunting when you think about it. One of the UF mottos were "Go Cure Cancer." And I didn't feel like I could ever uphold that end of the bargain to help with that cure. So I continued on with this fake plan...The ones all my Caribbean people told me to go after...The stuff that would make money they said...

If you know this life then just nod your head in agreement.

I continued the Sports Medicine journey nonetheless. Mind you, I wasn't good at science either, but somehow, I graduated. I finished UF with the APK degree, but if I wanted to do physical therapy I would have to take organic 1 and 2, Chem

1 and 2. And a slew of other classes that would probably have

me pull my hair out.

After finishing UF, I flashbacked to that one time I met a massage therapist at the UF. They attended this school called the Florida School of Massage. I figured I would go there as it would add an edge to me becoming a physical therapist. I know I wasn't great at science so I figured this was my way of making

some magic happen. Maybe physical therapy school would accept a scrub like me if I had a little more to offer. But going through massage school changed me. Here is the funny part, I had to catch 2 busses and walk a mile to get to school. After some time, I had a homie who would take me, but it sure felt cool to say the 2 busses and a mile thing. It felt like a story that a great great grandparent would tell his kids and the story would continue to get passed on from generation to generation.

But per usual there was something bigger. I went to massage school again because of my mom. When she was going through Breast Cancer one of the things I always had to do was give her a massage. She would yell like a proud Jamaican woman would, "Allleeeexx, come give mummy a massage."I would grab the big bottle of Jergens and put a whole bunch of lotion on her back and rub my little hands and elbows to get all the places that she said was hurting her. The chemo took a lot out of her. It was the one thing that soothed her. Back in the day I thought it was called a masseuse. But fun fact, massage therapists hate to be called "masseuses" (It has a negative connotation so remember that for future references). But she was the reason for it years later. I felt that if I became a massage therapist it would at least make up for the semi let down of not finding that cure for cancer. Even with Foolies, I figured I could honor her one more time with a tee during the month of October. I would give the funds to the cause of Breast Cancer. But to be honest, even that felt like nothing. Giving my money to some big foundation just felt like nothing after some time. Who is this going to? Who am I helping? Or am I just fattening somebody's pockets? Who knows. But I remember the moment that broke me. I remember a good friend buying some of the breast cancer awareness tees to a friend who was battling with breast cancer. I was writing letters to my customers at the time and remember writing that letter to her friend. Just saying to be strong, keep going, trust God, and just never give up. I felt good.

Until I reached out a few months later and found out that the friend had passed away. I mentally fell apart. Once again, what good was I even doing with this stupid T-Shirt

company?

Despite all the emails of people saying "your company helped me." Despite the messages about how the brand "Changed my life." All the calls and texts about what I have done and yet I still felt defeated. To be honest, every single day I feel like I am not doing that much. All I am doing and all the team may be doing is a bunch of motivational posts and an occasional T-shirt from time to time. Yeah, we have gone viral. Yeah, we have done some great things. But it is just T-Shirts.

And every time I get down and feel defeated I keep that little girl in mind. I keep the fact that my mom died while chasing her dream each and every day. I keep it all in the forefront of my mind. The moment I lost that hope I shut this cookie operation down. Sidenote: I've always wanted to find a reason to say that. One more check off the bucket list! (Laughs hysterically).

Another big picture of course as many all know is making it to the Ellen Show. Why Ellen? Well, she has a big heart just like me. Probably one of the biggest of them all. And she is able to do things for people that I could never ever imagine. In my mind maybe I just hope to get in her good graces not so I can just be on one episode with her and be a thing of the past but to learn from here if possible. And yes, her platform reaches millions. And God willing when the little red light on those big cameras go on and I am sitting in those chairs with her and she asks me why I am doing this I can drop the dopest and most amazing message to dreamers and game changers everywhere. I hope to be somewhat of a poster boy for every young black kid in the hood of Miami or whatever respective hoods they are from that lost their mom and didn't have much of a father figure. The kid that got told that they would never be shit. Sorry for cursing, but these were the things that I was told. For the kid that got told they would never make it out of middle school or high school. I just pray I don't end up crying too much and can't get my message out.

Last but not least, I need to also make sure these student loans are taken care of. I don't think I can do presuming as a mild-mannered Peter Parker and only having a day job. So hey, having my own business is a way to try to change my life around and the life of anyone else I've encountered seems like a good place to start.

I imagine one day getting a call from Ava Duvernay and she asks if I would be willing to fund her next movie. Without even asking her what it's about I say yes and cut her a check for whatever she needs. I imagine (still even though I kinda sorta but not really hung up the rap gloves) speaking and/or rapping on stages in front of ten of thousands. I want to create scholarships for low income and minority students. The list goes on and on...

These are the things that keep me going. My heart beats a little differently from my friends. With all these goals and dreams in my heart I figured I have a lot to fight for. At a minimum, it's a fight for the person reading this book to keep going. Who knows if I'll succeed at everything. But I'm gonna try. The beauty is that I'm not alone.

I think you get the point of this chapter. Latch on to the one speckle or speckles of hope and never let go.

See you in the next chapter. Make sure you connect with us on the gram as well! @Foolies. I would appreciate you connecting with us and shooting me some love!! Frfr.

Here's your Mission: Take five minutes to pen something to Facebook for me. Hashtag it with #FooliesApproved or even tag me if we are friends. Share with your friends why you do what you do. Tell them about some of the hardships in life that got you to this point. Now this may be a little bit deeper and more intimate but once again, this is what I've done for years for free and it really works. Is there a failure you can share? Is there a moment in life that was your turning point? Share it today. Stop thinking your words and your thoughts don't matter. If it's a long post you are good. You can blame me. Even start it off with saying "Nemo, told me to do this so I'm sorry y'all…" and then write your heart out. Don't want to do a long post? Then do a video. Go live on IG and just do that thing or say that thing that God has had on your heart for years now. This could be the moment that changes someone else's world and how much did it cost you? Nothing.

CHAPTER:-9

PATIENCE IS A TRAP

I am not here to talk to you about waiting and how your time will come. I am here to tell you about the exact opposite. Patience is a trap. I've always made this joke about patience. Patience is a virtue, but if you keep being patient it will hurt you. Don't worry, you have never heard me say that before and that is cool. But, it is a joke I have made for years.

Most people are waiting for absolutely nothing. We have created fake time lengths on our goals and dreams. Everyone is waiting to be called or led to do something. I didn't get a calling to start a t-shirt company. I didn't call to be super talkative and active on social media. I wasn't called to make Friday videos. That you can watch on Youtube by the way (slow wink...check out Foolies Fridays). And things will not get any easier. Things will not get easier. Things will not just magically workout. You will get your a** handed to you. People will betray you and people will turn their back on you. Your bank account won't always reflect the goals and dreams you are going after. But the definition of perseverance is going through things even though it gets tough. Even when it all gets overbearing and you hate life and everything around it. That is NOT when you give up. And the reason why you aren't where you should be is because you keep putting "TIME" in the equation.

At the moment I am no millionaire. I don't have some fancy house that I live in. I don't stay in a gated community. I have no real connections to make it or get to where I need to be. But, that hasn't stopped me. And salute to the few homies who have graciously let me sleep on their couches. A few others that sent me Publix gift cards in the tough seasons I appreciate you all as well. To my friends who not only let me grab a couch but let me crash with them for a few months while I got it all together. Now in my little ole 4 bedroom apartment with little to no resources I still make things happen. Using my cellphone and a MacBook I got because of school and doing whatever else I can with whatever else I have.

I remember being at this Indian restaurant with someone I looked up to. I was passionately telling him about how I wanted to change the world. And how this company Foolies "Inspiring people to foolishly live out their dreams no matter how crazy things may seem," was my answer to things. And how I was doing that through T-Shirts and people were really starting to catch on. With all the passion in my soul it didn't stop him from sucking it out of me. "Who do you think you are Gandhi? You can go back to India with all that change the world talk." What I wish I would have said is, "Well, I don't want to be Gandhi. And he was also a very racist man. If you had used Google instead of trying to be a smart a** you would have known that and I WILL CHANGE THE

WORLD SO TAKE THAT!" That is not what happened. I ran out and cried. I gave myself one of those crying headaches and when I could gather myself together I went back in and acted like nothing happened.

And I am sure you will be told by very important people that you suck and you can't do it. And how your ideas are stupid and no one will ever believe in that. But the "important people" won't be investors and/or someone on Shark Tank. It will be your mother, father, teacher, best friend, and/or maybe even your girlfriend or husband.

Plus, I can list a long dirty laundry list of people who should have let life stop them but they didn't. But even going back to my mom. She is the reason for the perseverance you see in me. She put her family on her back. She would take any extra income or goods she had and we would pack up barrels and send them back to Jamaica as much as I can remember. She was a beast. She would come home after work and make sure things around the house were done. I was a latch-key kid so I was home most times after school. Scared after every bump and thump until my mom would get home from the salon. I was 6'4 in my heart but at the time I still needed to stand on a chair or a footstool in order to wash the dishes. I would try to keep the house clean for mommy so that when she got home she could just rest. Many nights she would barely be able to do much other than to eat something and then lay down. She never let anyone see her sweat no matter how tough it got. She kept her bible by her bedside. You would have thought she highlighted every single page and every single scripture. She had faith and hope in me. She was training me to be a man and a husband. That was what the massages were for. That's what all the hard work she was putting in was for. So that I see the examples and would be able to lead on my own as well. If she never gave up even until that very last hair show she was in then why the hell would I?

And let's be honest. You didn't just buy this book because you wanted to support me. At least not all of you. You probably bought this book so you can figure out what the hell am I actually made of and figure out how you can muster up that kind of energy for yourself. Well 9 chapters in and I hope you have at least figure out somewhat how I am wired. And the biggest thing I would want you to realize is that whatever I am doing you can do it too.

So get laser focused. Stop bullcrapping (clean version). Give yourself a time limit. 2 years to success. And start grinding like nobody's business. You don't have to wait ten plus years. That's a farce. You can do it in half the time or less. Get with it and stop tripping!

Here's your mission: Start that one idea you have been putting off today. Yes, today. Find the smallest step of that dream and do it today. Even if it's just research. The hardest part of this game is starting. Have an idea and don't know what to do with it? Research someone else who has done it and how they started. Reverse engineer what they have done and figure out how you can do it in a way that makes sense for you. Now, at some point you may have to start investing something. If not money, then time. So if you are not willing to block out 15-20 minutes a day for your dream then I don't know what else to tell you. Get serious about your dream, homie. I can't want it more than you. And I can give you all the free gems, but if you do nothing to make a change in your life then you can't blame me, your mom, or anyone else. You gotta get deep in your gut homie and say these words: I never wanna be in this place again. Stop working for how bad you want the dream. Think about where you are and how much you hate that. Lisa Nichols (a virtual mentor of mines) was broke and living in a 2/2 or 4/4 apartment. It was her and her son. She was so broke that she had to wrap her son in a towel for a pamper. She said she never wanted to be in that place again. Now she's making millions. Not because she wanted some big dream. But because she hated her situation. Do you hate where you are? Time to change it for the better.

CHAPTER:-10

I WANNA SEE YOU WIN

My mom was a God-fearing individual. Anything and everything she ever did she led with that. So all I can imagine is that the only reason I am who I am today is because of her constant prayers. She gave it all so I could be safe. She gave it all so I can be a great man. She gave it all for her friends and family and anyone else who she came in contact with. Therefore, I will take that same energy and apply it to this business and anything else I put my name on. The disclaimer: I am not the hardest bible thumper in the game. I can't quote every scripture. But I know I truly wouldn't be here without God. From near-death experiences. To literally being inches away from being out on the street. But I won't make my situations any tougher than anyone else's. I just know I shouldn't be here. And I also need to keep that in mind if I ever get in my feelings. Or if I ever call myself getting down and wanting to give it up. As I have said before I wasn't called or "LED" to sell T-Shirts. But this vehicle has brought me here today so we will ride this wave for as long as humanly possible. So seeing you win is my birthright, my priority, and why this book after all this time is even being written.

But in order for ME to truly want you to win, I have to explain how I have lost as well. Just so we don't have a long drawn out story here are my moments of failure:

I never became a Physical Therapist. After college, I didn't have what it took to get into PT school. I didn't even bother taking those post back classes because there was no way I could ever get through those science courses.

I ended up working at an AT&T after college. Wasn't really putting that Applied Physiology and Kinesiology degree to use.

I think I graduated with a 2.9. I barely scraped my way out of my UF career.

32 years old and nothing to my name. No home. A raggedy car that I love, but it is raggedy. I can't even afford to get certain parts of it fixed at the moment.

Not married either. One day for sure, but I am getting up there as well. Women aren't the only ones worrying about age in regards to bringing little ones into the world. And I am tired of my Jamaican judgemental peeps coming at me sideways cause I have produced grandchildren for them.

I have written another book before. 2 before this one. Have you heard about it? Maybe. Possibly. But as you can see that didn't do any good for me either.

The first 5 years of Foolies I failed. I wasn't really making money. I wasn't really making sales. Even still today I can't act like we are balling out of control. You would think now as we are going into 7+ years and beyond we still haven't arrived. A few features, but what do I have to really show for it per se?

Failed rap career. I am not on the billboards. Never even got featured on any big rap blogs. No one knew about the man called Alexander The Great (ATG).

I've applied to be an MTV VJ didn't get it. That was back in the day, but it still hurt. I've applied to a few 30 under 30s and now I am moving on to 40 under 40s.

Another list of issues:

Fear

Anxiety. Been battling with this for a few months. Some days I can't even function.

Loneliness. Without an immediate family, I don't know. And since I haven't developed more than a real relationship with a few cousins I really wouldn't know where to start with trusting or building with absolute strangers at this point.

A WHOLE lot of DOUBT. Yeah, I say I want to be on The Ellen Show but please believe I have NO CLUE as to how it will happen. Hope and a Prayer.

I've slacked on my health. A lot of poor choices have led me to a few issues. High blood pressure being one and I just pray I get it under control before any others come together.

Lots and lots of loan debt. 100K plus. No blame, nor am I mad. Just being transparent.

I could go on and on and on. And my list of issues comes nowhere close to a lot of people. But why do I share this? I share this because I don't want you to think that the man in the Spiderman mask or costume is invincible. I am human. I get shaken up and worried and filled with sadness, like every other human being on the planet. Even with all the motivation, I spew I still have my second guesses. Some of you may read this and say these aren't real issues. And if so, then that's good. And that means I could look at your issues and maybe even say the same thing.

Either way, you now know my issues. Let us add some extra stuff of insecurity and immaturity and a few other things as well just to make sure you get a full dose of the truth.

But wait, Nemo. I thought you said you wanted to help us win? What was all that birthright talk in the beginning? Well my friends the way to win is through vulnerability. At least that's what it is for me. The way to win is through looking at all your crappy little issues and fighting back. So until you look yourself in the face and have a real convo about your crap then things won't get better. I repeat, things won't get better if you don't take a second to look at all your junk in your trunk. And I ain't talking about a big booty if you catch my drift! Sorry, I am corny. This is also a truth I hold as well (sticks tongue out).

I feel so sensei like right now. Wax on. Wax off. Breathe. Woosah. Water. Empty your mind, be formless, shapeless, like water.

Being honest, this mission is a selfish one. I am selfishly doing what I never got growing up. I wish I had someone lifting me up constantly. Yeah, there was one or two but negativity was a lot heavier. My environment at the time was trash and it didn't always fuel me as I needed. At some point I let the negativity and hate drive me. I let the idea of proving people wrong drive me. I let all the wrong things be my guide. I started to feel like I could do things on my own and remove God from the picture. Now mind you, I am still working a full-time job. I still freelance as an audio engineer and a graphic designer. Yes, I am truly Jamaican. And if you know you Jamaicans you know how us honest, loving, faithful brothers get down! Hahha! We work hard!

So now, here are your gems:

Become a conversation starter. Leaders start the convo. Ask questions that you would want people to ask you if they were interested in learning more about you. Being shy can be a strength, but you have to know when to switch it up and get the conversation started.

Get your Inner Gangster Up. Which means pop your collar. Keep your head high. Walk with a diddy bop no matter how lame you feel. This ideally means get your confidence up. And talk to yourself way better. A Gangster doesn't talk down to him or herself. Always treat you like the A-1 Steak Sauce that you are! Or the Yum-Yum sauce. Or whatever Sauce tickles your fancy.

Start being insane. See insane has a few meanings. The one I prefer is the one that means you are insane to chase the things that matter most to you. You have to be. A sane person wouldn't want to help the world. A sane person wouldn't want to open their nonprofit. A sane person would chill. A sane person would just remain comfortable. To do anything outside of the norm is an insane (to some degree) mindset. A lot of people told me "Are you crazy?" And you can insert any assortment of phrases after that. But if you think that you can approach your goals and dreams from a logical and rational sense then you my friend have already lost parts of your sanity. This company isn't called Smarties. It is called Foolies. Meaning you are foolish enough to go after the dream no matter how crazy it may seem.

Get the right data inside of you. I am talking about everything from the food you eat to the shows you watch to the things you consume. Every single day you deny yourself. You deny yourself the ability to grow. You think because you have grown in age that you have grown. No my friend, you are still the immature 18 year old you are in a larger or taller frame. You stopped reading. You stopped eating right. You barely drink any water. You stop experiencing life. We are pretty much walking and talking computers. So every single thing you add to you is like an applications. Some applications will help you run more efficient and effective. Others will serve as a virus. Care about yourself and the people around you enough to want to do better.

Stop doing the minimum. Stop paying the minimum on your loans. Stop paying the minimum on your credit cards. Stop doing the bare minimum at your school and your job. Stop doing the bare minimum at the gym or in regards to your health overall. Stop doing the minimum in your faith and with everything else as well. You are doing and thinking that because no one sees how out of place you are that it won't catch up to you. Get aggressive about the things you need to do to take care of yourself. You been doing the minimum for far too long and look where that has gotten you? You know you can do more. So do that.

DJ. Next track, please...

P.S. I wrote this part of the chapter as I sat in the heart doctor's office. A check-up to see what might be going wrong because I've felt a little off for a few months. I'm probably the youngest person here. This is another spark needed to realize I need to get it together. If I'm here I want to be because I chose to get a check-up. Not out of fear and panic. Because even then change won't happen. It will be temporary and short. But going forward things will be changing. Because due to my negligence I am here. It won't happen again.

Here's your mission: No junk food today. Pick one day of the week to not eat crappy. If you are going to eat out then find some healthy alternatives. Or, don't get an entire meal. Just get a sandwich or something. How does this change the world you say? The healthier you are the better you are for the people around you. Also, get some rest tonight. Sleep is a game changer. It helps with weight loss, stress, and even bringing down your heart rate. Having you around a lot longer can help your family and loved ones have something to keep kicking for. So let's make sure we are here for the people we love most. Time to make some life changes.

CHAPTER:-11

THE RESOURCES, WEBSITES, THE GEMS, AND HOW YOU CAN GET IN THE GAME WITH ZERO IN YOUR POCKET

A lot of the moves I have made have just been me hurling concepts in the air and hoping it lands in the right spot or on the ears of the right person. Cold calls. Emails. Networking events. You name it. If I could call my next book the Broke Man's Guides To Success then I definitely would make this the opening chapter.

How did I start Foolies? I printed the word Foolies on a dirty white tee. Made my friends wear it. Finally, someone said they wanted it. Took the money via PayPal through a random website I made for free. I also used a 3rd party T-shirt platform called Reverbnation. I am sure I mentioned that. I took the money I made from those sales and then invested back into Foolies. I am making this sound simple right? Yes, because at its core it is.

How did I learn about business? I found a website that was streaming business tips. CreativeLive. There was a course called the Personal MBA that was being streamed by a guy named Josh Kaufman. The guy told me to focus on the pain behind why you are selling your tees. He asked me (virtually) what problem does your company solve? That gave me the light bulb I needed to rethink Foolies. So I said hey, let me write letters to each customer.

Let me give them extra apparel every now and then. Let me call them. Connect with them. A few extra dollars spent to lose a shirt. But to gain a customer for life was worth it. Yes, now I have evolved and don't ship the teesmyself or package them up in the mini paint cans anymore because it became a physical load on me, but it helped.

I learned about the 1000 true fans concept somewhere along the journey. It was a free website that gave me a gem to focus on 1000 true fans/customers. Don't worry about getting millions of followers. Focus on the people who are already supporting you and have already purchased from you. I remember me and my COO discussing what would happen if we never had another customer again? What would we do? What would that look like? How would we behave? Between the thousand true fans and this question it helped us a whole lot.

Seth Godin (my virtual mentor) had a book I read called Linchpin. It was all about being indispensable. Cost me a few bucks, but it was worth it. The big question that woke me up was, "If you died today and all we had was google to learn about you, what would it say?" What would come up? If you died and all we could do is search for you on google what would you see? What I saw at the time was a spam account. It was horrible. My life would be belittled to a spam account. Nothing more. Nothing less. That made me change my mindset. I started to create and write more. I started to post more of my blogs online (I used tons of Google Plus when that was hot).

At the time I didn't have much money and all I could afford was this site called Bandzoogle. It was a site for artist and musicians. But now we have come so far with social media. There is a site called MEDIUM that you can use. It is free and it acts like a blog as well. You don't have to pay a single dime and you can start publishing your ideas and thoughts immediately. I am all about looking for ways to do things with little to no resources.

Canva was my baby for a bit. Think of a more generic version of Photoshop but online. Gimp is another free website that is a little more closer to Photoshop. You would have to download that one though. You all jotting this down? No worries. I am going to start getting to the strategy part soon enough.

Now outside of Photoshop and Illustrator, I lean on Snapseed and now I have just discovered an app called OVER which is now available for android phones. These are all apps to help you design and come up with concepts on a budget.

But with these apps, websites, and Youtube pages what does it even matter if you don't practice or put any of this into motion? What is the point if you don't begin to say to yourself, "How can I apply this?" How can I put all of this to work?" And after you put it to work you reflect and come back to your goals and your mission and repeat. The biggest thing you can do when building your business or your thing is to listen. To ask questions about what people really want. Before you go launching that idea or blog ask people the right questions.

For instance: You want to start a hair blog. Here are the questions you ask:

What hair products do you use?

What hair salons or stylists do you go to?

How much do you pay?

What kind of hair products do you use? Why?

Why do you love the hair brands you love?

What hair vloggers do you watch and why?

These questions help you get down to the need of what people want.

When you ask questions like "Should I start a hair blog?"

Well of course, everyone will say "YES!" And say "of course." But then you go putting out something that YOU want and not what THEY need. This is what I did to build Foolies. I got into the soul of what my customers wanted and needed. And every few months I do it all over again. Why? Because I need to 1. Confirm that people are on the right track. 2. Make sure I am not doing something outdated and that is not needed anymore. I guess 1 and 2 mean the same thing, but then maybe it doesn't haha.

But does any of this seem to need money? You have more than a hundred plus friends in your cell phone, right? Boom! You can start surveying and asking questions to the ones closest to you and then try hitting up the others later. Just be honest and tell them why you are calling. If they get upset or angry it is all to the good. If not, then you golden ponyboy. But you will never know until you try. If you don't want to call people then make a few FB posts, twitter posts, and Instagram posts. Talk to people at work, school, and in your communities. Then you take that knowledge and you SERVE THE HELL OUT OF YOUR AUDIENCE.

LISTEN. WATCH. OBSERVE. People say one thing and they do another. It is just how we work. So just keep your eyes peeled. Hit up sites like Alltop that map out all of the popular stories and headlines all over the globe. See what the general population is saying about your subject of choice. Then decipher that and break it down and then figure out how to deliver your content.

Roberto Blake, Tom Bilyeu, Tim Ferriss and Lewis Howes School of Greatness have been reference points as well. A few more like Shameless Maya, Devon On Deck, Peter Mckinnon and the list goes on and on and on.

And I can give you more blogs, more podcasts, and more resources, and more books, but what would it really do for you if you don't apply yourself? The goal after reading things for me is what is ONE thing I can implement daily? What is one thing I

can implement before the month is up? I follow and study

people. What people do. How they do it. I love talking to kids and the youth as well. I ask them what is hot, what isn't? I asked them what are they listening to? What are the kids wearing and talking about these days? I pick their brains because they just consume content all day. So I listen to them as well. Just to get a general idea of what they are doing.

THE LIBRARY!!

THE MOST UNTAPPED RESOURCE OF THEM ALL. If I had the time or the energy I would call every Library in the country. I would ask them what kind of resources they have in their library. Then I would jot it all down and make a website. THELIBRARYISYOURFRIEND.COM or something like that. And post everything from recording and editing equipment, workshops, and any kind of extra stuff that they may have to help people who have no money or on a budget find a library in their city that has the tools they need to be great. When I was a kid I remember when I didn't have a computer at my house and would have to catch a bus to the nearest library. Took about 30 minutes to an hour but I had to get my work done. When I was at UF we had this place called the CSE Lab. They had every freaking thing. Photoshop was all I needed at the time. We also had another place known as the Architecture Lab (Arc Lab for short). I would use Final Cut or Adobe Premiere. Don't remember which one they had, but I used it to make videos back in my hay day at UF. I just refuse to let anything stop me. If you are in college find out where the resources are on your campus. If you are not in school then find out where they are in your city. And hey, if you gotta UBER or catch a bus then make moves, not excuses. Also, download the Libby app. It allows you to access library books straight from your smartphone. For the free-ski.

I haven't used the site yet, but I plan to. Borrow Lenses is the name of the site. You can rent gear and equipment on a budget. Rent what you need. Make the money. Flip that to your advantage until you can buy the gear. Find a production hub in your city and see how much it would be to rent gear and equipment as well.

Sites like Social Media Examiner taught me so many nuggets on what is new in the space of social media as well. And please don't sleep on tweets, DMs, Facebook messages, and comments in the Youtube section. Sometimes you can simply ask people what are they doing to achieve or reach greatness and they happily pass you the book they read that helped them or share a gem with you that may change your whole entire life. Big brands like Herschel Supply, WWE, and so many others inspire me as well. I look up Instagram design pages for tips. I look at dope accounts that have great layouts. I have even started following HASHTAGS. Yes, you can follow hashtags. I am sure this is not new knowledge. If I like a particular tag or theme like Typography or, Photoshop Tricks I want to see anytime those things pop up to use that to my advantage.

Now, outside of a few books I may have recommended and a few classes that are probably under 100 bucks how much money have I told you to spend? Basically, nothing. Time and energy is what you have and you should use that to your advantage.

The thing is, I can only take you to the fridge. Can't make you open it and realize there is endless supplies and amounts of food for you to eat inside. Also, find a communication tool that you and your friends can use together: GroupMe, Slack, Email threads etc. Another small and free game changer. Watch content of videos you like and critique. Shoot, make a show out of it. Go to (my virtual friend's) Sean Cannell's page and learn you something about great cameras to start using for your

Youtube channel. If you keep strolling through his content he will give you the affordable stuff as well. He tries to help as many people in the different financial places that he can.

A lot of what you face is procrastination. If you could just kick that habit you would be good. Do a little bit of planning, creating a routine, and keep alarms and accountability buddies all around you. Don't be so hard on yourself and remember that even when you don't want to, it is probably best that you do.

A lot of times I am faced with not wanting to do stuff, but whenever I make it happen I am always grateful later.

Have a little ingenuity and keep a little bit of childlike naivete and the world is yours my friend! Oh yeah, sign up for my daily email as well. I drop tips, gems, and share my mistakes every single day. And then on Fridays, I hit you with more gems and resources as well.

Also, a good book to learn how to Copywrite better. It's called, "This book will teach you how to write better" by Neville Medhora.

One more thing…

HARO.

I use it to get ahead in life. You can try to do the same as well. It stands for help a reporter out. They send me a long list of things that one could write about. If my submissions are dope then they may get used in different publications. I've quietly gotten myself featured in Yahoo and a few other smaller publications as well. Quietly racking up the street cred. Forgot who put me on to this site, but it was a game-changer as well. Now, you may be discouraged if your work doesn't get featured, don't be. Because after some time if they don't get featured you can flip the content and use it for yourself on a platform like Medium or something.

One more thing...Masterclass.com! Such an amazing investment. I get no money for hyping any of these people or things up! Classes from Timbaland, Annie Leibovitz, Herbie Hancock and many others really helped me. Even the Serena Williams class on playing tennis helped me out tremendously. Do I wanna pick up a racket? Nah! I wanna learn from the woman who caused a racket by using one! Everyone becomes my fuel to continue being great!

Alright, you did it…

Last chapter!!

Curtains Close.

Last Call.

Watch Me Ball.

Spalding, To all yall!

Oh, I also want to thank the Black Panther Score/Soundtrack for helping me get through this chapter as well. I use music as my motivation to put me in a certain mindset when creating and writing. It's a simple game-changer. Dj, drop the final track! Before you get to the end...how are you feeling? @Foolies let me know you are almost done with the book! It would mean a lot! Also, hit me up if you want even MORE resources. I gotchu!

Here's your mission: Did you see something in this chapter that was helpful? Share it. Do you know a friend who may benefit from one of these links? Pass it on to them. Free of charge. They were already given to you so just give it away to someone else.

Also, set reminders on your phone with the phrase: "random acts of kindness." When it pops up you gotta do something. Write a letter, buy someone lunch, or any of the things mentioned in the book so far. If you are in a store and see something your friend mentioned they needed in their apartment or know your friend loves a certain restaurant and you see a gift card while you wait in line? Buy it and give it to them next time y'all see each other. Or, buy a gift card on your next trip to target and tell the cashier to give it to the next person in line. Seems pretty foolish right? Then do it!

Once again, we assume that this changing the world stuff needs to be Mark Zuckerberg building Facebook or solving world hunger. If you got real deliberate with your actions it would be a game changer.

Maybe you are working a great paying job and wanted to do a little bit more? Here's your idea: Pay A Bill for someone or, Cash App them money for lunch. Get on your Facebook page and ask if anyone has ONE bill this month they would like to be paid. Tell them to drop their name in the comments section and the bill statement. Then you will choose ONE bill to pay. Simple. Or, you can do the same thing and when they drop their Cash App info you can send them $10 bucks for lunch. You can do that once a month. Easy. Especially, if you got it.

Here is another idea:

Do you have a business book sitting on your shelf that you have already read? Can you share it with someone else? Maybe at work you can build a library that your coworkers can benefit from? Seems simple, but it could be a company wide idea that changes the entire office. I've seen it done at my own 9 to 5. Or, just say "Hey, I am giving away my book about this business

subject, or my Harry Potter collection (I know, that may be tough but do you really need it just collecting dust?)." Maybe the person who needs it can use it for themselves or their little ones. Now the person you share that Rich Dad, Poor Dad book with can benefit from the knowledge inside it that you have already obtained. That is why I noted that this is "Kinda-Free." You have already spent the money on the books. You have already read them and consumed them. Now give it away. If you do this at all just tag me, or use the hashtag #FooliesApproved. Hey ya'll I'm giving away these business books I will even cover shipping and then take a picture of your books you may be giving away. Simple as pie my friends. Don't overthink making an impact.

One more idea: Do you have a bunch of friends that are business owners? Invite them over to the house for lunch. You can cook it yourself or you can have it catered. Tell them that the reason for the invite is that you wanted to have business owners over to meet and connect. Simple, right? This may run you possibly $50-100 bucks? If you already have the food at the crib then maybe nothing at all. You could be making waves by just bringing people together. I think you get the point.

CHAPTER:-12

I'LL NEVER GO BACK TO SCHOOL AGAIN, BUT THEN I WENT BACK TO SCHOOL...

Now I know college has a bad rap right now. But, just hear me out. Now, I am not telling you put on more debt. I am not saying that college is the end all be all. But, here are the upsides I think that school can provide.

Preface: I am no baller. I don't have mommy and daddy. Don't have a trust fund. Don't have some random piggy bank with an oasis of money. So for me, I am not coming from this space of having it all.

I needed to go back to school to open up some extra doors for me. I didn't have the connections I needed and so I went back to school to learn Audio Engineering and then a few years later Graphic Design. I needed the skills to break into these industries and I personally would not have been able to do it via Youtube and reading books. I needed a curriculum. I needed structure. I needed to be able to connect with professors and industry pros. So I decided to go back to school for these things. These things have opened up my eyes and ears more than any piece of advice I could give you.

Now this is if and only if you use every single thing that the school you attend has to offer. Most times people will just go to class and go home. So if you are going to go back to school then follow these rules:

For me, I take advantage of my professors. Why? Because I didn't do this at University of Florida. I only talked to professors when I was failing a class. The other part was my pride got in the way. My pride made me stay to myself even when I needed help. My pride made me keep my hand down when I should have been asking questions I didn't know about. So when I went back to school again I made sure every single chance I got I asked for help. I sat down in teachers' office hours. I asked the tough questions. And I picked my professors' brains outside of class. I didn't just ask them about school work I talked to them about life.

What are big mistakes that young engineers make that you constantly see? They would say things like "When you're young everything is loud. Don't put too many compressors and plug-ins on their mixes." For those who don't know about audio let us interpret this in a way you understand. When you are young and in your profession don't be so quick to do everything. Don't be so quick to use all your fancy tools to do your job. Yes, you have learned a lot in school. But the basics are always needed to be applied. Plus, experience matters. Your experience will help you do things and gain access to people, clients, and connections you didn't know were possible. But you have to be willing to humble yourself and learn. I would dig deep into anything suggested to me.

A Full Sail Grad and friend, Leslie Brathwaite, gave me some great advice before graduating. His credentials are ones I admire greatly. So far in his life, he has worked with artists like TLC, Akon, Jeezy, T.I., Beyonce, Jay Z, Migos, Cardi B, and Rihanna. In his early days he's worked with TLC in the early 90s and even work with Michael Jackson and Whitney Houston. Like I said, his resume is impressive, and his knowledge has always been valuable. He shared these tips with me one day:

Take time off. He mentioned that he didn't take enough time off when first started. He always felt like he was going to miss something. Taking time off gives you perspective, He said. He wishes that he took more vacations earlier.

Young engineers (professionals) talk too much. Just shut up and (do your job) push the buttons.

He mentioned to always involve yourself in creative things. It doesn't always have to be music (or things in your profession). It could taking pictures, editing family videos, and/or anything that keeps you creatively sharp.

School will teach you the technical stuff. A mentor will teach you about life. Find a mentor if you can. That will help you level up in your industry.

I asked him these questions back in 2012. If it wasn't for me being in school I would have never been able to ask him that piece of advice that I have used to open up doors for me in my industry today. I still lean on this grad for advice today. And even though we don't talk every single day I listen and watch the advice he shares with other students and other industry professionals.

For me, my UF family is the reason why my brand is still alive and probably why I am still alive as well. My friends have helped me with everything from having a couch to crash on when I couldn't afford an apartment. When I was building this business and didn't have food in my fridge my homies from UF helped me out. Because of me going to school in the first place I gained a family. My fraternity gave me another great sense of family. My brothers taught me how to tie a tie. They opened up my eyes to what it is to be a man. The frat taught me how to plan events, how to be efficient. They stressed the 7p's. Proper Prior Planning Prevents Piss Poor Performance. Learning poems like The Man Who Thinks He Can and Invictus are still poems I recite 10+ years after I became a brother of the frat.

See for me, without school I would have never made it out of the streets of Miami. I would have been trapped forever. I had to get up and leave my hometown to see the possibilities. Foolies wouldn't have happened. The number of people I have been blessed to impact wouldn't have happened. I touched a lot of lives in my UF days. Not being cocky or arrogant or anything. I just had an incredible experience during my time in college and despite the fact that I couldn't pay for it all on my own without government assistance or loans it was the only way that I could make it. Other people may not need it and they can find ways around it, but I wouldn't be the mind I am without not only going to school once, or twice, but then a third time.

I went back to school for Graphic design because I got tired of not knowing how to make Foolies look like how I wanted it to look. Also, when Foolies becomes this super huge company I want to be able to talk to my art team and give them concrete steps to make things better. I didn't want to be the boss that just complained that things were "ugly" or "just not it." I want to be able to give them the tools and steps to get better because I know the industry. Also, since my first degree in audio engineering, I got into a lot of cool stuff thereafter. I've worked for Digital Marketing Agencies (took that gig to learn about how to write and to learn about SEO stuff) Freelancing for companies like ESPN3, working as a stagehand for live bands, concerts, and then a whole lot of volunteer work for my church as well. That is where I took on another career switch up and started to become a lighting engineer. So more skills just kept getting added to the belt. Then I said, why don't I just learn graphic design as well to make everything whole. I know audio, I am learning the lighting industry, and with graphic design, I could be even more powerful as well. This final school journey helped me in a lot of ways.

Oh yeah, I went to massage school as well. That was a personal move and bucket list thing that I did for my Mom. I wanted to be the husband she trained me up to be and I remember massaging her when I was little and wishing I knew how to help ease the pain away to the point of no return. So even though I didn't become a doctor and learn how to cure cancer, massage therapy seemed to fulfill another purpose. All in all, I am a Jamaican. I have a lot of skills under my belt that has helped me with not only connects but compassion. These different industries helped me become more empathetic. I learned how to hustle and how to make a name for myself every step of the way. All of these experiences make up the man who runs this company. Some people may say it is all random and call me stupid which they have. But, once again, the man you see is a hybrid of many things.

For some, you can learn all this stuff on your own. No school involved. But for others, going back to school may be the only thing to help you level up and get to your next and best level. It may cost you some change. But at some point, you are going to have to pay to play. If not in school in some other way. With your time, your energy, and who knows what else. I wanted to improve my connection game. School became that playground. I did everything I said thus far I would do. And now I hope to use these skills I've obtained to revolutionize the entertainment field in an amazing way. So thank you Full Sail University. For being one of the first places that believed in my dream and gave me the tools to do so.

Hopefully, I am officially done with school after this last degree. I never want to see school again. I also wanted to do graphic design back in my UF days. I just thought Sports medicine was the thing because my Jamaican family members kept insisting it upon me. So I was trying to appease people and make them happy. Telling people I was an Applied Physiology and

Kinesiology student always made people "ooooooo" and "aaahhhhh." No one ever questioned what I was going to go with that. But for some reason with my Audio and graphic design degree, they always have questions. I've been able to impact more lives doing these two things. I've probably seen more money in these professions of entertainment as well. People forget that entertainment has been around since the dawn of time and that people will always pay to escape. ALWAYS. Movies, Video Games, Music, Technology etc. No one ever hears about those industries being in a "recession." Now thanks to social media getting into these worlds are even easier than ever. And no, the game is not saturated. You just need those 1000 true fans that I dropped the link for earlier in chapter 11. I always knew that this is where I should have been.

But, I didn't listen to myself. I didn't trust my gut. I let everyone get into my head. When I finally started listening to me I found happiness. Happy I bumped my head so many times because it finally led me to the goal and to where I was supposed to be.

I think that is it, for now, my friends...But there will be more greatness to come. I just hope that this helped. I really hoped that my perspective added to yours. And hey, if you don't like or agree with anything I have shared then that is okay as well. Your path is your path. Everything I shared in this book could lead you to your demise and you may have your own way of doing it all. Just be prepared to make some sacrifices. This book may have made things seem like it was easy. But I tried to wrap my 30+ years of knowledge in this book and I still don't think I have done enough. But...I won't start to beat myself up...I will leave it here.

Outro: Lay Low Homies!

Get these pesos!

Hit some people you love with the Besos!

Peace!

If you have made it this far and want to support me even more you can hit our Foolies Merch Shop/Sign Up For Our Daily Emails, and Watch Foolies Fridays in the same stretch.

When you make your purchase of your tee send me a screenshot or something so I know it's real!!

I'd love to see where you go next because of all of this!! Keep me posted. As you get to another level drop the #FooliesApproved hashtag and tag @Foolies as well. We want to know what is happening out there! Okay...

Here's Your Mission: You may have a degree that you have never finished. Not sure of the reason but IF you said that you were going back to it at some point and haven't then ask yourself what happened? You may need to get back to that.

If you have a degree and have said that you were going to get your Masters or PhD then I think it's time. You have put it off long enough. Now, if you have your dream job then cool. But, if you know you need to make that move then please do so. Stop being lazy and go apply to that school you have been meaning to apply to.

If you are reading this and saying, "Nemo, ya boy can't afford college. Sorry man, but miss me with that." Okay, fair. So what you about to do family? If you are not going to go to a physical school then how will you supplement your learning? If Youtube University is your option then great. Now, I need you to double down and start making a curriculum of all the things you would have wanted to learn from that University and then go research it on your own. Use the Masterclass site I suggested. Go to

Linkedin Learning/Skillshare and pay for whatever their monthly membership is. If it's business, marketing, branding, etc then reach out to the company you want to work for and tell them that you will spend a year working for them for free. Or, could I shadow you on the weekends when I am not working? Or, could I swing by after hours? Because not getting the degree can't be the excuse. Can't be a Doctor? Maybe an X-Ray Tech? Maybe there is a position under the one that requires a college degree that you can learn about and possibly gain entry or access into.

What you can't do anymore is make MORE excuses. At minimum, start learning business. No matter your industry. You can do that for free. Or, for a few bucks you can buy some of the books from authors I have mentioned. If you are THAT broke then go on Youtube and type in the name of the book you want to read and I promise it will be there. If not, then type in the name of the book followed by the word "summary" (Linchpin Summary). Maybe the small gems from the summary can help you out. Or, find a class/course and split it 4-5 ways with your homies. If ya'll can pass around ya Netflix account info then you can do the same for a business course. Got it? Then good!

Hope you have accepted each and every mission given throughout this not so perfect body of work. Changing the world won't be easy. But, it doesn't have to cost an arm and a leg to do it. It may mean you have to suck it up and work on that Youtube series after work. It may mean you have to deal with working full time and doing your photography thing on the weekends or whatever day you can. At some point you will have to make a sacrifice of your own.

Last message for the homies:

I really do pray and hope this book found you at the time that it should. I pray you walk in the spirit of boldness going forward. I pray you leave fear behind you and release the shackles you have put on yourself. You were put here for greater. You were put here for more. You were put here for something more profound than what you may be doing currently. I can't commit to that statement fully. Cause you may be doing extremely well...But, if you know there is more for you then I pray you find the way and the opportunity to get there. But faith and prayer is cool and all but without the work behind it then it's really just you playing ya self. And we don't want you doing that. But, you don't need to be a celebrity, have tons of money, or any other bells and whistles to shake up the world or leave your dent in the universe. You got a story from a simple guy who has just finessed every single thing whether I was scared or not. I wrote this book scared. I self-published it scared. And I will have more dreams I chase while still scared or in fear. This book isn't here so you can be fearless. But if it can teach you to FEAR LESS then I have done my job. Got it? Great!

Leaving you with another set of gems:

Below will be a couple of quotes I've made over the years to post to social media. Just figured you can get one last sip of motivation before you wrap things up: Tough Questions that need to be asked every single day.

WHAT ARE YOU WILLING TO DO TO MAKE YOUR DREAMS COME TO LIFE?

WANT TO CHANGE YOUR LIFE?
UPGRADE
YOUR
STANDARDS

YOUR DREAMS

WON'T WORK UNTIL YOU DO

STAY AWAY FROM
ENERGY VAMPIRES

THERE WILL NEVER BE A RIGHT TIME

STOP TRYING TO HAVE IT ALL TOGETHER

THE MONEY WILL COME.

JUST KEEP WORKING ON CHANGING LIVES.

HIT PUBLISH
PRESS RECORD
MAKE THE POST
FINISH YOUR BOOK

PICK
YOURSELF
DON'T WAIT ON ANYONE TO CHOOSE YOU.

@FOOLIES   #FOOLIESAPPROVED

YOU WERE
GIVEN
THESE
GIFTS AND
IDEAS FOR
A REASON.

Study your heroes influences, not your heroes. - Pensado

#FooliesApproved

"If you want a million dollars, Be willing to help a million people." -

Paul C. Brunson

What are you thanking this year for?

What will you be hoping for in the New Year? Holla!!

I did it mom. Hope I made you proud. Your Babushka.

Dear God, you put every single word on this paper.

I can't thank you enough for using me.

Not sure where I would be without you.

Let this be the beginning...

FOOLIES APPROVED:

How to change the world with a foolish dream and zero in your pocket

By Alex "Nemo" Hanse

Made in the USA
Middletown, DE
03 January 2020